Generative AI and the Future of the Humanities

Dana J. Gavin

Generative AI and the Future of the Humanities

Reading, Writing, Teaching, Labor

palgrave
macmillan

Dana J. Gavin
Writing Center
Dutchess Community College
Poughkeepsie, NY, USA

ISBN 978-3-032-06533-9 ISBN 978-3-032-06534-6 (eBook)
https://doi.org/10.1007/978-3-032-06534-6

This Palgrave Macmillan imprint is published by the registered company Springer Nature Switzerland AG
The registered company address is: Gewerbestrasse 11, 6330 Cham, Switzerland

If disposing of this product, please recycle the paper.

Competing Interests The author has no competing interests to declare that are relevant to the content of this manuscript.

Contents

CHAPTER 1

The Luddite's Battle Cry

Abstract This chapter introduces the main argument of this book: namely, that while generative AI presents a unique threat to the acquisition and development of critical reading and writing skills, it also represents a general public malaise to those skills. The humanities as a professional institution have not been able to break through the public discourse noise to make a case for the necessity of those skills. This book aims to raise questions, offer suggestions, and ultimately argue for action rather than passivity.

Keywords Humanities · Critical reading · Critical writing · Generative AI

> A system of machinery almost organic has been devised and arranged, which, while it relieves the human frame of its most laborious efforts in printing, far exceeds all human powers in rapidity and dispatch. That the magnitude of the invention may be justly appreciated by its effects, we shall inform the public, that after the letters are placed by the compositors, and enclosed in what is called the form, little more remains for man to do, than to attend upon, and watch this unconscious agent in its operations.
>
> (John Walter II, qtd. in Moran 1973, 108)

D. J. Gavin, *Generative AI and the Future of the Humanities*,
https://doi.org/10.1007/978-3-032-06534-6_1

> This is merely to say that the personal and social consequences of any medium — that is, any extension of ourselves — result from the new scale that is introduced into our affairs by each extension of ourselves, or by any new technology. (McLuhan 2013, 19)

Introduction

In late November of 2022, I likely heard about ChatGPT on the social media platform known then as Twitter. I was not nearly as interested in current technology as I was in learning everything I could about the late eighteenth and early nineteenth-century innovations for the steam-powered printing press. That research was critical to my dissertation, and I was trying to keep my head down, pressing forward through muddy writing to a final graduation-deserving document. Still, I followed Academic Twitter, and the buzz finally reached my fingertips.

Sitting in my office in the Dutchess Community College Writing Center in Poughkeepsie, New York, I opened ChatGPT (like many, many, many other people at the very same time, I imagine) and wrote a prompt question based on my current literary concerns. Unfortunately, I did not save that query and response, but it was something along the lines of looking for examples of Imperialism in Wilkie Collins' *The Moonstone*. Within seconds, an effective answer had been delivered to me, as a cucumber tea cake on a silver tray. I was stunned, then bereft, then filled with gallows humor; I carried my laptop out into the lobby of the Writing Center and showed ChatGPT's work to my colleagues. "Start polishing those resumes, folks, we're going to be closing up shop here," I moaned dramatically.

I wallowed for a few days, and noted, imprecisely, how often I encountered mentions or discussions surrounding ChatGPT. In short order, I realized that I was hearing an echo—the anxiety and anger I had been reading about for years at that point, voices from the nineteenth century reacting to the advent of the steam-powered printing press, was being replicated, now in my hand as I scrolled social media on my smartphone. I also became more aware of the company behind ChatGPT, and of the roles that Elon Musk, Peter Theil, and Sam Altman in the founding of OpenAI; I listened more closely to the way this product was being foregrounded, inescapably, into my daily information consumption.

My wallowing dried up, and a hot anger replaced it.

In November 2022, New York State was nearly two years past the lockdowns stemming from the COVID-19 pandemic, a time when many academics across the world were forced to take their well-honed pedagogy into a purely digital space (and for many of them, it would be their first time in a such a space). My academic circles were filled with English professors, and so I was consumed with how to translate freshman composition into this asynchronous class space. I was fortunate: I had experience teaching online, asynchronously, before March 2020. I did not have experience managing the social and emotional fallout from a global health crisis that devastated my students, my colleagues, and myself. Emerging from the intensity of 2020, as we started to trickle back into something like a pre-COVID-19 educational existence, the wounds were deep for many educators. Complaints were voiced in person and online about how many students either plagiarized papers or fully refused to do the assignments. Stress and frustration dominated the cultural and academic mood, in my perception, and in general, people were simply worn down to exposed nerve endings.

I do not presume to speak, as it were, for the humanities like the Lorax speaks for the trees; people who teach in the humanities have tongues and have been speaking up—or rather, *writing up* for a very long time about the existential dangers we have been facing in education. One of my goals for this book is to draw from many strands of conversations in and out of academia, about the humanities and about public life, from those embedded in technology fields and those well outside. I hope this book can provide a conversation spark in the veins of reading, writing, teaching, and labor discourses, so that we might feel like we are comrades in the fight on all fronts—not in a fight against AI specifically, but in a fight against a mass illiteracy event. My professional experience in the classroom has largely been in rhetoric, composition, and literary studies. I have been fortunate to have interdisciplinary bent to my education and research, and I feel a profound commitment to disciplines that teach critical thinking skills through reading and writing as the pedagogical core. My attention has long been in this space, and as the director of a Writing Center, I feel even more aligned with educators outside of the English discipline, supporting folks who are also using writing as a primary assessment source.

To my mind, ChatGPT simply broke the written-assessment educators' hearts. It was one indignity too much. Perhaps I broke too, a bit, under the weight of book bans in the United States, under the successful 50-year assault on public education, and under the anti-democratic deluge of misinformation that rolled over me and my students like a tidal wave of sewage.

Instead of being sad, I got mad. And I thought about winemaking.

In October 2017, a series of wildfires took root in Northern California; one of the most destructive of the many fires was called the Tubbs Fire, which burned through wine country, including Napa and Sonoma counties. When the grapes were harvested for the purpose of making wine, they were infected with what scientists call “smoke taint.” The grape skins had absorbed the smoke from the wildfires, attributable to climate change. The resulting wine from the 2017 harvest tasted of smoke and ash, nearly unpalatable. As Sigfredo Fuentes, Associate Professor of Digital Agriculture & Food Sciences at the University of Melbourne, noted, “While flavour characteristics caused by the soil, plants and environment are the source of the variety we appreciate in wines, these spoilage characteristics certainly make the wine less palatable for wine lovers” (Fuentes et al. 2019). Wildfires, enhanced by man-made climate change, produce clouds of toxins which seep into the pores of the grape skins, altering the taste and quality of an indulgent intoxicant. The wine is often undrinkable, and is often disposed of, as it is unfit for sale.

I was sitting with roiling fear, anger, and a resignation to the idea that the discipline of composition, and English in general, was going to be irrevocably changed. Much as winemaking is an ancient practice, a creative craft passed down through generations, so too is writing a craft passed down, when it is most effectively taught, from the more practiced scribe to the novice. I sensed the end of a practice I cherish greatly, and that I feel is crucial to personal development—that is, writing, in my experience as an educator and as the director of a community college writing center, is the key to unlocking deep learning and deep critical thinking, both of which aid in self-actualization and in full societal participation. In both cases (of wine and writing), something external and man-made had come to poison the process that crafters had been honing for ages. The situations seem hopeless, as the ensuing taint seems inevitable.

Yet I quickly came to realize that, maybe, there were people interested in profiting off my fear and anxiety, and I began a great pivot. The discussions we are having today are in no way unique—we have lived thinking that the next generation doesn’t know how to write, or that the technology they use is corrupting their ability to think and write critically.

What we are up against, now, is that these very old conversations are happening at a crisis made of an obsession with speed and the degradation of labor; a crisis which is further fueled by the effects of a pandemic. And yet, I am filled with sincere hope that our disciplines will finally be forced to revise ourselves in ways needed for at least 50 years.

That sincere hope has been challenged, regularly, by people within and without academia. In the very early days, there seemed to be great fear and anger over the emergence of technology that seemed primed to allow students to avoid the difficult labor of writing. "The College Essay is Dead" proclaimed *The Atlantic*, December 6, 2022, as the headline for an article written by Stephen Marche. Rashi Shrivastava, writing for Forbes, suggested "Teachers Fear ChatGPT Will Make Cheating Easier Than Ever" on December 12, 2022. "Teachers are on alert for inevitable cheating after release of ChatGPT," wrote Laura Meckler and Pranshu Verma on December 28, 2022, for *The Washington Post*. My personal conversations with fellow educators echoed the spirit of these headlines.

Quickly thereafter, however, a new strain of extreme optimism emerged: on April 6, 2023, Will Douglas Heaven's article, "ChatGPT is going to change education, not destroy it," appeared in MIT Technology Review with the subtitle, "The narrative around cheating students doesn't tell the whole story. Meet the teachers who think generative AI could actually make learning better." On February 29, 2024, Forbes published Jeff Fromm's article, "Can AI and ChatGPT Reshape Academia: Arizona State Believes So." The backlash to the backlash had begun in earnest. Indeed, I have perceived in academic conference settings, educator workshop settings, and on multiple social media platforms, that an ardent strain of toxic positivity flows through and around conversations. It feels utterly fair to see educators adopt this radical optimism—"if you can't beat 'em, join 'em" is a powerful mantra. If, after decades of being on the receiving end of abuse and financial cuts, humanities folk both want to be perceived as technologically progressive change-makers and get a piece of the financial windfall that seems to be dangling from OpenAI's business model, it is difficult to sneer at such a response. It is, of course, disagreeable to be considered close-minded, a human roadblock to happiness and prosperity, a stick-in-the-mud, and, most offensively, a filthy Luddite.

Reclaiming the Luddite

For most of my life, I have considered the term "Luddite" a derogatory one. I have striven to be the sort of open-minded person who is willing to try new technological advancements, in the hopes of not being "left behind." My formative years coincided with the arrival of personal home computers and was, blessedly, well before social media platforms emerged. As an academic who has buried herself in nineteenth-century literature, I am keenly aware of the concept of relevance and, especially, the perception of lacking it. And yet, it is precisely my research into the past, into the publishing technology of nineteenth century Britain, that has enabled my pivot from fear and frustration to resolute resistance to Silicon Valley's party line. In popular culture, the Luddites were frustrated craftsmen in late eighteenth-early nineteenth century England, who, in a fit of rage, smashed all of the fancy loom equipment that was being used to make linen and stockings, as the loom machines were taking jobs away from the red-blooded English weavers and textile workers. Luddites resisted progress because they were selfish, greedy, and small-minded, obviously.

What if, possibly, that was an inaccurate portrayal? Researchers have made compelling arguments regarding the actual motives and activities of the Luddites, painting them less as a regressive monolith opposed to technology, and more as a strategic response to their mill and factory owners' greed. Certainly, in "Luddite or Technophile?—Policy Preferences for Governing Technology-Driven Economic Change," Jaewook Lee offers a full-throated rebuttal: "While the term 'Luddites' is often saturated with pejorative connotations with technophobe images, the movement reflects those who voiced against disruptive consequences of labor-saving technology and [who voiced support for] widespread demand for socioeconomic equity and morality in economic order" (Lee 2024, 1–2). Mill and factory owners looked to cut costs, so they purchased loom machinery and hired inexperienced laborers, who could be paid far less than skilled craftsmen. The results—poor textile craftsmanship, the undermining of skilled laborers, the reckless and unsafe work environments—were an anathema to the textile workers who had spent their lives cultivating their craft and their relationships with vendors and customers. Gary M. Anderson and Robert D. Tollison (1986) get into the weeds of the poor craftsmanship issue in their article, "Luddism as Cartel Enforcement," describing how "cut-up work" was the most critical offense committed by the mill and factory owners. First, notably,

Anderson and Tollison explain that the men who made up the Luddite rebellion also used loom machines—they were not anti-technology in the least. They were protective of the quality of their work, however, and of their profession as a whole. Unscrupulous hosiers, who relied on unskilled workers manning machines, produced "cut-up stockings," which "were manufactured from large pieces of knitted material, assembled on large frames where they were cut out and sewn in the shape of a foot. Such stockings were less durable and generally of poorer quality than the traditional stockings, but were relatively cheap and increasingly popular among consumers" (Anderson and Tollison 1986, 733). Customers may have been happy to pay less for these stockings, but the craftsmen believed that their profession would ultimately suffer if customers became disenchanted with stockings that fell apart far more quickly than they used to. The Luddites were motivated to course correct and restore a higher level of craftsmanship to the process.

The Luddites approach to dealing with this professional threat was severe, and I believe that is why they have loomed large (no pun intended) as these iconic figures. The image of enraged craftsmen violently smashing machinery is perfect for a mill or factory owner who wants to portray themselves as the victims of an unsophisticated mob. Note that the strategy worked then and continues to work now! Reality bears out quite differently, though, and that image needs correcting. Luddites did smash machinery, but their actions were not at all indiscriminate. According to Anderson and Tollison (1986), "Throughout the literature it is acknowledged that 'good' and 'fair' hosiers were conscientiously spared and only the 'unfair' and 'hard' hosiers were targeted" (733). Luddites did not object to the machinery, they objected to bad bosses and bad business practices. If they had only objected to the machinery, we would not be talking about them 250 years later. No, they raised hell in defense of their craft and their craftsmen being undermined under the guise of "saving time" and "profit," and the mill and factory owners were not about to let the public catch wind of this worker-rights-first attitude. Thus, Luddites were painted as mindless, spineless, technophobes, rather than strategic resisters to the corporate party line that "saving time" was essentially and always an indication of virtue.

Returning to the waning days of 2022: I went back to read about this corrupted wine phenomenon that I'd recalled encountering years ago and learned that researchers have proposed mapping solutions: "These models combined with affordable geo-referenced NIR spectroscopy measurements of berries could allow growers to map contaminated areas of a vineyard to facilitate decision making at harvest" (Fuentes et al. 2019). Fuentes et al. (2019) reported, "Spatial maps of smoke contamination can also help to achieve differential harvests to avoid mixing fruit with smoke-tainted fruit." Mapping is, in fact, the key to understanding not only how the advent of generative AI as a mass-accessible tool is impacting (and will impact) the writing and reading process, but also illuminate the process through which generative AI has come into our lives in the way that it has. I believe that mapping out the process that has produced tools such as ChatGPT is key to understanding how and why generative AI is having certain impacts on reading, writing, and critical thinking.

My mapping effort is grounded in assemblage theory, as realized in Jane Bennett's (2010) theory of vibrant matter: all matter—human and non-human—is perpetually interacting with each other, influencing and being influenced, propelling and retracting, processing towards products (which, in turn, are part of process to more products). Assemblage theory delivers a framework for how to see the disparate materials that are in conversation with each other, especially when thinking of assemblage as a verb rather than a noun.

One way to imagine assemblage is to think of a collage, or the bringing together of disparate items into one harmonious product. For example, one could think of the steam-powered printing press, and imagine all of the components and their provenances: iron must be harvested by men in the north of England, coal must be obtained beneath the earth's crust, laborers with unique skills must endure great physical hardship to produce these materials, inventors from different nationalities must contribute innovative designs in order to bring forth this great, hulking, pulsating, dirty machine that ultimately enables an expansive literacy that shores up a white supremacist national British ideology. German inventor Friedrich Koenig is generally credited with inventing and producing the steam-driven cylinder machine in 1811: in *Printing Presses: History & Development from the 15th Century to Modern Times*, James Moran (1973) describes Koenig's cylinder machine thus: "it carried a single cylinder, not a pair, and of quite different structure to the heavy pressing roller. It was hollow, and acting as platen and tympan [a pad], impressed the paper on the inked forme in a rapid, sharp motion and not with a long crushing effect" (104). Koenig's invention was overlooked by many, but in a visionary move, John Walter II, owner and editor of The

Times, realized that the cylinder machine could revolutionize his production. Moran (1973) notes, "Walter accordingly ordered two steam-driven, double machines for The Times, to be ready in twelve months, with the proviso that none were to be sold during the lifetime of the patent within ten miles of the City of London" (107).

The steam-powered printing press's reception attests to the churning political and financial machines: printers and publishers marveled, while workers threatened violence. Thus, Walter had his steam-driven machines installed in secret and began printing before the workers were even aware of the installations. Walter printed a notice in the first steam-printed edition on 29 November 1814, which describes the process thus: "A system of machinery almost organic has been devised and arranged, which, while it relieves the human frame of its most laborious' efforts in printing, far exceeds all human powers in rapidity and dispatch" (Moran 1973, 108). Notably, the announcement declares the machine "a system," acknowledging that the press is made up of many parts and is quite large, as well as that it is "almost organic," perhaps a balm to the nerves of those laborers who see the rise of machinery as a threat. The announcement reckons with the human intervention still required: a human "devised and arranged," even though the human is rhetorically absent from the sentence. This almost organic system acts for the benefit of the human frame (less organic than the machine in this telling). McLuhan (2013) argues that "it is the medium that shapes and controls the scale and form of human association and action," be it labor or play (20). Thus, the machine does not eliminate jobs—it "relieves" men from difficult labor, and "exceeds" their capacity, specifically here in terms of speed (a repeated theme in this project). The technology enables a situation in which production, and labor, are scaled up beyond the scope of human capacity, producing a new reckoning of time for humans for different labor and different activities, time that once was accorded strictly to labor for production.

The announcement goes on to insist that the public appreciate how removed from the process men are (and yet, it inevitably demonstrates how humans are still very much involved), by detailing the process steps—identifying the relationship between material and worker, and between material and material; the final blow to seeing this assemblage as balanced is, however, the final sentence in the process description: "[L]ittle more remains for man to do than to attend upon and to watch this unconscious agent in its operations" (Moran 1973, 108). The unconscious agent supplants humans and yet represents incredible human achievement. The machine should protect humans from deadly elements; however, it is seen as hurting people. Thus, the printed announcement—an assemblage itself—reveals how contemporaries were already conceiving of the relationship between contributors, human and nonhuman as well as nonhuman and nonhuman.

The workers responded to the introduction of the new steam engine printing press by threatening "destruction to [Walter] and his traps" (Smiles 1890, 169). According to Moran (1973), "[...] Walter entered the press room and astonished the men by telling them that the newspaper was already printed by steam; that if they attempted violence there was a force ready to repress it; but if they were peaceable their wages would be continued until similar employment could be procured" (108). This dramatic scene demonstrates the "psychic and social effects of media," as McLuhan (2013) describes it, of the machine medium. McLuhan (2013) argues that people are often unaware of the "psychic and social effects of media," ignoring what he calls "the nature of the medium"—"that any technology could do anything but add itself on to what we already are" (23). Identifying and focusing on the content of the medium is a distraction; rather, analysts should attend to the impact the medium has on the people in its sphere.

So, what of the impact of generative AI on the production of knowledge in the humanities, if the generative AI tool is an extension of ourselves? Generative AI and the steam-powered printing press have a great deal in common, from the point of view of assemblage theory, as both are vibrant assemblages of human and non-human materials. The assemblages of coal and iron, like the steam-powered printing press as well as trains, introduced speed to the lives of Britons, and that speed made it possible to people to move faster, to create things quickly, move goods and ideas around faster, and to give the impression of fortification.

Generative AI also impacts time, pace, and scale, as generative AI tools mimic knowledge acquisition and deployment, by gathering information from a variety of sources and cobbling it together into a collage of "new material." Generative AI is an assemblage (of assemblages). First, an assemblage of raw materials: we must imagine and source how generative AI is formed, what raw materials come together to create generative AI. We know computers and databases use rare, mined minerals, for example. In the case of OpenAI, they committed human rights abuses with their use of Kenyan workers employed to refine the program (as detailed in Billy Perrigo's January 2023 article for Time titled, "OpenAI Used Kenyan Workers on Less Than $2 Per Hour to Make ChatGPT Less Toxic.") Experts warn that increased adoption of and dependence on AI has serious environmental consequences: for example, "MIT has reported that the cloud [data storage and processing in remote servers] now has a larger carbon footprint than the entire airline industry, and a single data center might consume an amount of electricity equivalent to 50,000 homes" (Marr 2023). Generative AI must be trained with increasingly larger and larger datasets, and Marr (2023) reports that, according to MIT Technology Review, "training just one AI model can emit more than 626,000 pounds of carbon dioxide equivalent—which is nearly five times the lifetime emissions of an average American car." That is calculable pollution that impacts the growing effects of climate change.

The scope of the generative AI pollution crisis feels overwhelming, and the many challenges brought to the fore by generative AI require people to slow down and critically assess a multi-layered reality. However, the very concepts of critical thinking and reading are, frankly, under attack—not strictly from generative AI tools, but from people with an impetus to undermine such learning. If that seems hyperbolic to declare, let me offer a few examples: the erosion of trust in the scientific community, and trust in expertise, has led to outbreaks of historical illnesses like polio, once thought conquered. In the United States, anti-vaccination advocates enjoy political successes tied to the ignorance and suffering of others. All it takes is one person with a TikTok account going viral—free to them, deadly to the rest of us. The mechanisms of information sharing have not created the absence of critical thinking, but they have dramatically impacted the speed (time) and the scope (pace) of how misinformation flows. As such, time and pace play important roles in the way I think we fight back against the rising tide of uncritical living.

And yet, if we ask students (and our colleagues) to slow down, to take their time, to learn critical thinking and writing skills first and polish later, we are asking them to go against the culture in which we live. It is a radical ask, especially if students have been using apps and algorithms in K-12, and because our culture tells us all we must move faster and faster. Remember Facebook's original motto: "Move fast and break things." Again, I return to a question that is repeatedly knocking around in my head: who profits from this break-neck, break-back, break-everything speed?

Chapter Structure

Before we dive deeply into the relationship between time and speed, I take up writing in Chapter 2, "Through a Glass, Darkly: Generative AI and Writing," from the perspective of novice writing and professional academic writing. Many conversations (taking place on social media and listservs) are drifting into broader discussions of how pedagogical "best practices" might evolve to meet this twenty-first century moment. Some have been arguing for this evolution for a long time and perceive the current anxieties over generative AI as a perfect opportunity to reassess what we do as educators, how we do it, and how we measure it. The process by which generative AI tools generate texts can inspire us to think about the accumulative and derivative nature of scholarship, which believers of the "lone genius" myth (and its companion, "original thought"), loathe doing. That reckoning, I argue, is invaluable, as we might grapple with perceiving our scholarship as part of a stream rather than believing it must stand alone when it simply cannot.

I argue that generative AI has a deleterious effect on literacy in Chapter 3, "Making Bricks Without Clay: Generative AI and Reading." When I think of people encountering generative AI as they are trying to gain reading literacy, or improve their reading skills, I shudder: reading requires a level of trust that the author is acting in good faith, yet AI is essentially untrustworthy. That is, when I attempt to read words on a page, part of what guides me and what sustains me is a belief that the author of the text is trying, in good faith, to put forward something coherent. I may disagree with the concepts presented, but the letter and the words are arranged in a manner that I believe is intended to communicate a complete thought. Generative AI doubles down on literacy disintegration by obfuscating authorship—the assembling of knowledge—as it scrapes the Internet to crudely construct texts, contributing to a long-evolving attack on "expertise," where "doing my own research" means watching dubious YouTube videos on any number of subjects that require extensive professional development to master. In an article titled "How AI Can Distort Human Beliefs," Celeste Kidd and Abeba Birhane (2023) write,

> [P]eople assign agency and intentionality readily […] people commonly read intentionality—and humanlike intelligence or emergent sentience—into generative models even though these attributes are unsubstantiated.

> This readiness to perceive generative models as knowledgeable, intentional agents implies a readiness to adopt the information that they provide more rapidly and with greater certainty. (1222)

Kidd and Birhane (2023) argue that generative AI's writing is declarative with no caveats, suggesting a level of certainty that is unwarranted. This misplaced faith is made more malignant given that generative AI represents a polluted assemblage of knowledge: the process of creating an AI-generated essays may illuminate negative aspects of some types of scholarship practices such as colonialism and theft as it scrapes the Internet, fails to cite sources, commits labor and human rights abuses, and creates environmental pollution. We know there are traces of attributable scholarship, but those traces are hidden under layers of plagiarism and paraphrasing. This act of "standing on the shoulders of giants without naming them" recalls the politics of citation in general, where minoritized or marginalized scholars are often left out of current scholarship in favor of traditionally cited, privileged scholars. This omission has the effect of introducing bleach into a thriving ecosystem: the scholarly discipline is polluted by their absence, and given the role of scholarly publishing, those uncited authors may not be employed scholars for long.

Chapter 4, "And Then There Were None: Generative AI and Labor," will delve more deeply into the relationship between time and speed; throughout this book I am advocating for a lens that takes any suggestion of time-saving or labor-saving as suspect. That is, I advocate for a sensitivity to what I will call "incapacitating technocapitalism," if you will, which I define as technology being deployed for the enrichment of the few that also has a useful numbing effect. In his seminal work, *Understanding Media: The Extensions of Man*, Marshall McLuhan (2013) argues, "[The name 'Narcissus'] is from the Greek word narcosis or numbness. The youth Narcissus mistook his own reflection in the water for another person. This extension of himself by mirror numbed his perceptions until he became the servomechanism of his own extended or repeated image" (63). Coming to a greater awareness of the numbing effects of technology (and, critically, why we seek numbness in the first place), brings me closer to the "post-tech" concept: Sarah Genner (2016) writes, "Offtime [a digital productivity app that limits technology usage to emphasize work-life balance] defines post-tech (or post-technology, post-digital-technology) as technology that puts humans at the center and supports focus and intent, well-being and independence (from technology) instead of increasing mere productivity and time spent with digital devices and technology only" (162). We must reassess our use of technology, including educational technology, and consider how we are promoting the human capital first and foremost.

Chapter 5, "Sowers of Discord and Scandal: Generative AI and the Student/Educator Connection," offers an assessment of how generative AI pollutes the necessary labor in which educators and students engage in independently and cooperatively. Generative AI looks like magic, and we have poor language to describe the work it does, such as "intelligence" where there is no intelligence. And yet, our analysis of AI can draw our eyes towards chaos and filth. Pollution can refer to violations of purity and sanctity, to profanity and desecration; it can also refer to environmental contamination and the introduction of dirt, stains, and waste. Pollution is not a thing that happens outside our control. We create the situation, and others perpetuate it and demand that we buy their solutions to clean it up. In the case of AI, the creators have directly and indirectly caused the pollutive environment they now lament—the environment they are now asking us to pay them to remedy (plagiarism). We are also being presented with an opportunity to reassess our relationship with our students. We generally understand that it is counterproductive, pedagogically, to create an adversarial environment if we are trying to educate and inspire learning. To take advantage of this opportunity, we could start by considering the current environment. At the same time, companies fan the flames of plagiarism fears and try to sell us expensive software to solve the problems they are creating. We know that creating adversarial relationships between educators and students does not yield good learning outcomes, and here, we have the same companies who have created this obfuscation problem selling "solutions" to educators to establish surveillance states in their sacred classroom space.

It is also worth considering that some traditional pedagogical approaches were developed many decades ago for young white men of privilege, who had the luxury of reading, thinking, meditating, and composing with fewer impediments than students face today. I think often of William Wordsworth's (1966) sentiment in *Preface to Lyrical Ballads:* "[...] Poetry is the spontaneous overflow of powerful feelings: it takes its origin from emotion recollected in tranquility" (27). I struggle to find that essential time to think, to process, to reflect, and to compose, and so I know our students do as well. Educators can and must demystify and undermine generative AI's potentially disastrous effects on reading and literacy.

I return to the concept of "post-tech" in the final chapter, "Deep, Deliberate Engagement: The Way Forward is Through." Discussions of generative AI have centered around academic honesty, copyright, and equity. We must go deeper and broader. It is not hyperbolic to suggest that we are at the crisis' edge in terms of critical thinking and information literacy. Generative AI equips bad actors with accessible tools. I do not believe that submission to companies promoting generative AI is inevitable, or that courses cannot be changed. I think, though, that we must interrogate AI-generated content so that we can explain to students what this tool is and how it functions. We can use our investigations to learn more about our own scholarship, much in the way examining the steam-powered printing press offers a fascinating view inside the Imperial assemblage of the nineteenth-century publishing industry. We must become detectives, investigating the assemblages into which we are plugged, identifying the matter we are influencing and being influenced by, as far extended from our corporeal selves as possible. To accomplish this investigative work, we may rely on our classical liberal arts training as a model to use. We know that deep reading and writing processes are key—let us lean into that process as a method of interrogation.

References

Anderson, Gary M., and Robert D. Tollison. 1986. "Luddism as Cartel Enforcement." *Journal of Institutional and Theoretical Economics (JITE)/Zeitschrift Für Die Gesamte Staatswissenschaft* 142 (4): 727–738.

Bennett, Jane. 2010. *Vibrant Matter: A Political Ecology of Things*. Duke University Press.

Fromm, Jeff. 2024. "Can AI and ChatGPT Reshape Academia: Arizona State Believes So." *Forbes*. February 29. https://www.forbes.com/sites/jefffromm/2024/02/29/can-ai-and-chatgpt-reshape-academia-arizona-state-believes-so/.

Fuentes, Sigfredo, Eden Jane Tongson, Roberta De Bei, Claudia Gonzalez Viejo, Renata Ristic, Stephen Tyerman, and Kerry Wilkinson. 2019. "Non-Invasive Tools to Detect Smoke Contamination in Grapevine Canopies, Berries and Wine: A Remote Sensing and Machine Learning Modeling Approach." *Sensors* 19 (15): 3335. https://doi.org/10.3390/s19153335.

Genner, Sarah. 2016. *ON-OFF: Risks and Rewards of the Anytime-Anywhere Internet*. vdf Hochschulverlag AG an der ETH Zürich. https://doi.org/10.3218/3800-2.

Heaven, Will Douglas. 2023. "ChatGPT Is Going to Change Education, Not Destroy It." *MIT Technology Review*. April 6. https://www.technologyreview.com/2023/04/06/1071059/chatgpt-change-not-destroy-education-openai/.

Kidd, Celeste, and Abeba Birhane. 2023. "How AI Can Distort Human Beliefs." *Science* 380 (6651): 1222–1223. https://doi.org/10.1126/science.adi0248.

Lee, Jaewook. 2024. "Luddite or Technophile?—Policy Preferences for Governing Technology-Driven Economic Change." *Socio-Economic Review*. https://doi.org/10.1093/ser/mwae025.

Marche, Stephen. 2022. "The College Essay Is Dead." *The Atlantic* (blog). December 6. https://www.theatlantic.com/technology/archive/2022/12/chatgpt-ai-writing-college-student-essays/672371/.

Marr, Bernard. 2023. "Green Intelligence: Why Data and AI Must Become More Sustainable." *Forbes*. March 22. https://www.forbes.com/sites/bernardmarr/2023/03/22/green-intelligence-why-data-and-ai-must-become-more-sustainable/.

McLuhan, Marshall. 2013. *Understanding Media: The Extensions of Man*, edited by W. Terrance Gordon. Ginko Press.

Meckler, Laura, and Pranshu Verma. 2022. "Teachers Are on Alert for Inevitable Cheating after Release of ChatGPT." *Washington Post*, December 29. https://www.washingtonpost.com/education/2022/12/28/chatbot-cheating-ai-chatbotgpt-teachers/.

Moran, James. 1973. *Printing Presses: History & Development from the 15th Century to Modern Times*. University of California Press.

Perrigo, Billy. 2023. "OpenAI Used Kenyan Workers on Less Than $2 Per Hour to Make ChatGPT Less Toxic." *TIME*, January 18. https://time.com/6247678/openai-chatgpt-kenya-workers/.

Shrivastava, Rashi. 2022. "Teachers Fear ChatGPT Will Make Cheating Easier Than Ever." December 12. https://www.forbes.com/sites/rashishrivastava/2022/12/12/teachers-fear-chatgpt-will-make-cheating-easier-than-ever/.

Smiles, Samuel. 1890. *Men of Invention and Industry*. J. Murray.

Wordsworth, William. 1966. "Preface to Lyrical Ballads, with Other Poems." In *Literary Criticism of William Wordsworth*, edited by Paul M. Zall. University of Nebraska Press.

CHAPTER 2

Through a Glass, Darkly: Generative AI and Writing

Abstract Writing is such a funny, fickle activity, that often unites people in feelings of frustration and annoyance because it is a taxing endeavor if one takes writing seriously. This chapter focuses on novice (student and layperson) and professional (academic and public-facing) writing and calls for a reifying of the idea of public humanities, where we are addressing our communities-at-large as writers of all abilities and raising writing as a human right in a consistent, thoughtful, and compassionate manner.

Keywords Writing · Memory · Literacy · Generative AI

Introduction

What might it mean if people consumed information about writing like they consume information about retail commerce—how often are we bombarded with advertising for material consumerism, even when we are not explicitly shopping? I am being told what I should wear, what I should eat, and what medicines I should take every day. Can we imagine a world where messages about creativity abounded? I think about the early successes of a program like National Novel Writing Month (NaNoWriMo)—in 2015, 431,626 people, from 633 regions around the globe) participated, each aiming to write 50,000 words in 30 days. Let me note

D. J. Gavin, *Generative AI and the Future of the Humanities*,
https://doi.org/10.1007/978-3-032-06534-6_2

that the unhappy ending(ish) of NaNoWriMo highlights some serious weaknesses that we must attend do, but I will save that discussion for Chapter 4. For now, I want to focus on the idea that there are people who want to write, who want to join with other writers, and we can imagine opportunities where more people can see writing as both an activity of self-actualization *and* an activity that does not need to be commoditized.

Writing is certainly on people's minds, but often not for the happiest of reasons. Truly, people who are not even supposed to be talking about writing cannot help but bring it up, and yet, often wind up saying the most profound things. For example, the podcast "Too Scary; Didn't Watch," which features three friends discussing horror movies, typically begins with the hosts discussing something scary that happened to them recently. While listening to the episode where the hosts breakdown the film, *Bone Tomahawk*, I empathized with host Sammy Smart as she lamented, "The scary thing that happened to me this week is that I started writing my speech to officiate [podcast cohost] Emily and Joel's wedding […] you guys, writing is so hard. So hard. It's so hard. It's the hardest thing." Her fellow hosts, Emily and Henley, expressed solidarity, and then Sammy elaborated, "[…] writing specifically is my least favorite of that [creative journey] time because it's like, it feels so tied to your brain" (Gonzalez et al. 2024, 00:02:31–00:04:10). I don't tune into "Too Scary; Didn't Watch" to meditate on writing and composition theory, but there I was, driving home, listening to a novice writer express so beautifully why writing raises so much anxiety in most of us. Writing feels like a direct representation of our thinking—it is, as Sammy said, tied to our brains in a very intimate way. We are laid bare by the letters we string together. The podcasters went on to express feelings of inadequacy, sharing "[…] when you're making art, it's like sometimes you're like, this is stupid, this looks bad, or this is, but when you're writing and it's bad, you're like, I'm an idiot. I'm stupid […] Why does anybody like me when I'm this stupid?" (Gonzalez et al. 2024, 00:04:29–00:04:39). Having taught first year composition at four institutions, and now, early in my tenure as the director of a writing center, I have encountered this level of fear and despair year after year, with students who came to our interactions with strong skills as well as students who needed substantial support. The fear is tied to the inherent vulnerability embedded in writing as an activity that involves a reader decoding and interpreting, and, in so many cases, passing judgement.

The Question of Memory

Is it any wonder, then, when ChatGPT became widely available on November 30, 2022, that many writers of different stripes perceived a balm to the pain of writing? Writing has always required technology of some kind, be it a surface of clay, a sharpened stick, ink and quill, ballpoint pen, or a word processor. Some professional writers still write by hand, appreciating the slower pace, whereas others felt liberated by the speed at which they could translate thoughts to text using typewriters and personal computers. It is more than reasonable for writers to be interested in new digital tools, like Zotero and Scrivener, even as debates over whether these tools are truly time-savers rage on.

Fear of change is universal too. Socrates warned that writing would lead to education loss, in the form of losing the ability to memorize rhetoric and recite on command. It is difficult to argue with that charge, but the assertion does depend on the idea that knowledge rests in memorization, not in the ability to generate ideas. When I was in high school, in the mid-nineties, I had several phone numbers memorized: family, friends, probably my mother's office number. I recall having to memorize and recite soliloquies from *Hamlet* and *Macbeth*; even during my undergraduate years at Southern Methodist University, I remember shaking with nerves as I recited passages in Middle English in front of Dr. Bonnie Wheeler in the stairway of Dallas Hall for some exam. I do not remember any justifications for memorizing tracts for school—I believe I thought it was good, simply, to have certain well-regarded passages from The Canon at the tip of one's tongue. More specifically, I came to understand that plays in particular were for performing, not silent reading, and that everyone should get a taste of Shakespeare at minimum. Part of the appreciation surely came from the mouthfeel of the dramatic pronouncements. Surely there was also a bit of a feminist stirring, as my classmates at the all-girls Catholic high school I attended were proclaiming, "Tomorrow, and tomorrow, and tomorrow, /Creeps in this petty pace from day to day" with no male Macbeth actor in sight.

Of course, I had certain phone numbers memorized because I had to dial them, one key stroke at a time, anytime I wanted to call someone. Surely as a little child I had to work at memorizing my own phone number, but in large measure, that later memorization came from necessary repetition. Today, smartphone in hand, I can barely remember my own phone number, let alone any friend or family member's number.

I don't even see their phone number when I press a likeness of their face to call or text them. Maybe this matters little or not at all; am I really hobbled by a mind that is not routinely practicing memory-based activities?

To this end, a passage from Sir Arthur Conan Doyle's *A Study in Scarlet*, published in 1887, always comes to mind when I think about my mind's capabilities. Dr. John Watson has determined, much to his dismay, that his new flat-mate Sherlock Holmes knows nothing about Copernican Theory and, worst of all, claims that he does not want to know anything about it. In fact, Holmes declares that "[n]ow that I do know it I shall do my best to forget it" (Doyle 1887, 9). To a medical man, a learned and degreed man like Watson, this is tantamount to heresy. Watson goes on to note for the reader that, in his estimation, Sherlock Holmes knows very little about anything other than crime and areas that are related to the investigation of crime, and this astounds him.

Holmes responds to Watson's dismay with a useful description of the mind:

> I consider that a man's brain originally is like a little empty attic, and you have to stock it with such furniture as you choose. A fool takes in all the lumber of every sort that he comes across, so that the knowledge which might be useful to him gets crowded out, or at best is jumbled up with a lot of other things, so that he has a difficulty in laying his hands upon it. Now the skillful workman is very careful indeed as to what he takes into his brain-attic. He will have nothing but the tools which may help him in doing his work, but of these he has a large assortment, and all in the most perfect order. It is a mistake to think that that little room has elastic walls and can distend to any extent. Depend upon it there comes a time when for every addition of knowledge you forget something that you knew before. It is of the highest importance, therefore, not to have useless facts elbowing out the useful ones. (Doyle 1887, 9)

The brain-attic space is finite, and ideally, we are well-served by outsourcing the memorization of things like phone numbers, birthdays, anniversary dates, and such to our smartphones, our smart calendars with their helpful pop-up reminders. Thinking as Sherlock Holmes does, we should keep our brain-attic space tidy for the most urgent and pertinent information. To be sure, Holmes is not saying "be ignorant;" he is advocating for a radical and judicious use of memorization. Elsewhere in the Sherlock Holmes stories, we see the manner in which Holmes stores clippings and notes related to his past and current cases. His brain is no voluminous database—far from it. Holmes acknowledges his bodily limitations and, thus, urges an offloading of unnecessary weight.

What I find troubling in my life, however, is that I have offloaded too much, to the point where my brain is frankly less capable of memorization and even just memory retention and retrieval. The point of Socrates' admonition today may be less of an apocalyptic warning of impending idiocracy and more a caution that throwing out any skillset wholesale should be thoughtfully considered. Whenever this conversation comes up (and by "this conversation," I mean any of the iterations that have flowed from the move to written discourse, including and not limited to the use of calculators and the internet), the canard is shot down, suggesting that the warnings are hyperbolic and reactionary. "We don't need to learn algebra – we have calculators!" people cry. As a person who has a deep-seated fear of failing at math, I pull out my smartphone whenever I am attempting to correctly calculate a tip on a restaurant bill, for example. I am grateful for the calculators. I do recognize, however, that my brain is not better for my over-reliance on calculators for simple equations. We aren't talking about calculus here—we're talking about a percentage of an amount added to the amount. I think making my brain work a bit is wise, even though it takes time and, frankly, makes me uncomfortable. I need to keep those neurons firing in as many patterns as possible: research has demonstrated that learning mathematical skills significantly impacts brain plasticity, cognitive functions, and quality-of-life measures (Beddington et al. 2008; Zacharopoulos et al. 2021). If someone in my younger years had told me that the struggle of learning math would help my brain stay healthy, I might have seen it as more necessary and been less willing to give up.

Another conversation, closer to writing: "You don't need to learn to spell anymore, especially by memorizing words – that's what Spellcheck is for." We see this battle occur in classrooms too, over the use of laptops as opposed to people handwriting their notes or in-class work. The relationship between handwriting and positive reading and writing outcomes has been studied (note Ray et al.'s (2022) research on visual-motor memory (VMM) and handwriting instruction in kindergarten). Many argue that students should go back to handwriting as it improves memory recall for exams. This argument is fair, but it skips over a few salient points: first, students may no longer practice writing in K-12, as Chromebooks and tablets have become the norm. They may not even be good typists, as typing courses have faded out of fashion. Students may have other impediments to writing, such as muscular-skeletal disorders or learning differences that precludes handwriting—those students must not be forced into older technologies like pen and paper when we have machines and programs to support them. What I am suggesting is that a case must be made for why penmanship may be a worthwhile choice for many students (not all), and that the convenience of a digital device may be creating more challenges than it absolves.

This is the challenge and the crux of the problem at hand, and is why one need not even use the term "generative AI" when discussing the challenges to literacy and cognitive efficacy: what makes hard work attractive beyond a sense of self-drive? In "The Adventure of the Speckled Band," Watson writes, "In glancing over my notes of the seventy odd cases in which I have during the last eight years studied the methods of my friend Sherlock Holmes, I find many tragic, some comic, a large number merely strange, but none commonplace; for, working as he did rather for the love of his art than for the acquirement of wealth, he refused to associate himself with any investigation which did not tend towards the unusual, and even the fantastic" (Doyle 1892, 142). Obviously, the fictional detective does not live in a late-capitalism environment; would that we all were descended from country squires and the French artist Horace Vernet! His ability to glory in the work for its own sake is a distinct privilege, but it does offer a glimmer of inspiration when one considers the nature of motivation. It has come to feel self-defeating to tell some students that they should work in a particular way if they are able to, while never skimping on accommodations that allow other students an opportunity to enter the academic conversation. That is, if a laptop or tablet makes it easier for everyone to take notes, shouldn't everyone have the opportunity to use them, regardless of the gradation of need? Perhaps the salient question should be, if your gradation of need is on the relatively low end of the scale, are you short-changing yourself out of an opportunity to develop some necessary skill by availing yourself of the shortcut? For some people—for example, a person with dysgraphia—handwriting is a skill that cannot be attained, and assistive technology enables that person to move on to the next skill they are attempting to attain (such as, in the case of composition studies, a well-organized sentence or paragraph). A student who has the musculature and composure to write, however, should be educated on the potential values of making use of their options as they, too, progress towards the next skill to be attained. In thinking about accommodative technology in this way, we can avoid penalizing or stigmatizing students who need assistive technology to progress, while also demonstrating the value of interstitial skill building to those for whom the technology is more convenience than necessity.

The Necessity of Writing

At this point, I feel the need to aggressively make the case for writing as a skill, because I do feel that people give lip service to communication as a needed skill, but do not reward or make space for the development of the skill. Maybe this prosecution seems overwrought, hyperbolic, and unnecessary—certainly, if you, reader, have devoted your life to the study and teaching of rhetoric and composition, or a discipline within the field of English as a whole, you believe in your bones that writing is important. It is necessary, in fact, to achieve self-actualization. And yet, the world is doing its best to destabilize people's abilities to acquire writing skills, with the call often "coming from within the house," as the overseers of curriculums look for ways to reduce English and composition requirements. Many educators fight to keep those few required classes, knowing one or two semesters of first-year composition only scratches the surface of the path towards skills mastery, hoping that "Writing Across the Curriculum" concepts continue students' skills development down the mastery path.

What does writing do, and why must we continue to fight for it to be part of curriculums in higher education? Writing is a uniquely powerful mode of learning, as Janet Emig (1977) argues,

> [T]he symbolic transformation of experience through the specific symbol system of verbal language is shaped into an icon (the graphic product) by the enactive hand. If the most efficacious learning occurs when learning is re-inforced, then writing through its inherent re-inforcing cycle involving hand, eye, and brain marks a uniquely powerful multi-representational mode for learning. (124–125)

The "symbolic transformation" does not occur easily or naturally for most people. As Emig notes, speech is more natural and disorganized. The physical, mental, and emotional discipline to force the body to connect to the mind, to take hold of the technology and commit symbols (based on tenuous social agreements) represents an incredible achievement. Emig draws focus to the other important component—repetition and reflection. Oral communication exists in one place and space and cannot be reviewed unless it is captured by another media. Writing is self-reinforcing, as each word, sentence, paragraph, and composition represents a new opportunity to try one's hand at meaning-making that can be reviewed. Emig (1977) writes, "a unique form of feedback, as well as reinforcement, exists with writing, because information from the process is immediately and visibly available as that portion of the product already written" (125). The writer can then review the previous word, sentence, or paragraph, and either revise or gain wisdom on what was achieved. The writer is then in possession of a record of thought development, and the act of reading one's words, revising, rewriting, and writing forward represents a self-perpetuating mode of learning. The writer can consider, in this reflective position, not only the content of thought that has been produced and recorded, but also the process by which those ideas where recorded. A rich vessel for inquiry of the process and product has been produced even as learning has occurred through the production itself.

We can see academic programs using a writing-to-learn mindset in their pedagogies. According to Finkenstaedt-Quinn et al. (2021), in their study assessing Writing-to Learn (WTL) programs in STEM education, "WTL attends directly to enhancing content knowledge" (1548). In their paper, the researchers meticulously describe a program they developed at the University of Michigan called MWrite, that was integrated into the institution's learning management system (LMS) and both standardized and supported STEM educators to use writing as a method to learning. MWrite seems to have helped students with the dreaded peer review portion of the WTL program, working as a guide outside of class time to help students read and respond to their peers. More importantly to me, the researchers detail how much support is given to faculty, particularly in the art of formulating the prompts to which the students will respond. Teaching assistants called "writing fellows" are also a key component of this project, and the researchers describe the networks of faculty support (through learning communities and mentoring, among others), that last throughout the semester when a faculty member is employing the MWrite system. Finally, a debrief is conducted at the end of the semester to learn from the experience. British medical schools teaching palliative care are also incorporating writing-to-learn elements into their pedagogy;

researchers studying the efficacy of writing reflective palliative care essays at the University of Cambridge School of Clinical Medicine found that most students considered the writing useful as a method of contextualizing and processing their learning. As one student in the study noted, "I found the experience of meeting the patient very valuable, and it was useful to draw together what I had learnt in the essay afterwards. I think this will help the information and learning points to stick in my head" (Borgstrom et al. 2016).

The process described above can seemingly take place in isolation, but that is a fallacy—one of the most potent to disprove. Writing instruction must be present on some level, first to introduce the idea of symbols and recursive thinking. Everyone must be taught to write. Writing skills are then further cultivated by readers, who respond to the writing and craft to foster greater development. It is through our discussions about our own writing, our own processes (or lack thereof), and our ideas that we can hope to become more competent at writing through our ideas, writing ourselves into knowing, and writing to share our ideas with others.

Writing and the art of composition have never, and probably should never, be easy tasks, as they are essential to truly knowing oneself. Being in a state of full understanding—of oneself, one's thoughts and feelings, a topic, or argument—to the point of being able to commit one's thoughts into words with specific details is close to achieving self-actualization. The labor of understanding is frustrating. Even people who write professionally tend to talk about how they enjoy *having written* rather than engaging in the act of writing. Writing is difficult and clunky, and teaching writing is difficult and clunky. Writing as a means to understand what we know and what we think about a topic or argument is necessarily challenging work, which is why student writers often only realize the thesis of their paper at the very end of said paper. In this way, writing is a scholarly action verb that serves us as a process; as a product, writing is valuable as a snapshot of who we were at any given time in our lives.

Every generation has heard that they can't write, and every next generation of educators has complained that their heirs apparent cannot write. If the complaining is to be believed, few people if any have ever been able to write, ever in the history of recorded time. Obviously, there is a touch of the sensational and hyperbolic—one need only follow Paul Fairie and his incredible lists of headlines ripped from decades of print media to understand that there is absolutely nothing new about this variety of moaning and griping. It is not, however, unreasonable to notice a decline in some aspects of writing skill proficiency over many generations. It is fair and necessary to critically evaluate the pressures put on people, especially young people, that might stand in the way of students learning to become effective, confident, and committed communicators.

Much has been written about the role of standardized testing and its impact on education, and I will reference but not rehash that ocean of information. Just anecdotally, students in New York State recount learning how to write in a particular style favored by the Regents Board and admit during their first year of college (at both small private colleges as well as community college) that they feel unprepared for general academic writing, let alone writing for any other sort of purpose. Even students who report that they love writing demonstrate a lack of basic grammatical skills, though these are often the students so in love with language that they are hungry for direction for fine tuning their work. Students grow more and more resistant to the slowness of time necessary for writing (and reading). If it cannot be accomplished in one sitting or two, it is not an activity worth doing, and it is understandable why people feel this way. Every message sent to people is predicated on "grind culture," which includes the mentality that all actions should be in service of attaining wealth coupled with "work smarter, not harder." Writing, even in the best scenarios, is necessarily iterative if it is to be done well, and to serve a purpose; that is, you will write something that communicates some message, and someone, at minimum, will read it to understand. In the case of a personal journal, that writer and reader will be the same person, but the position is still different and thus, iterative in terms of consumption. The writing must at least be rung out twice. Even quick journal scribbling is not instantaneous. In truth, writing involves thinking, which takes time, choosing words to type out, correcting mistakes even quickly as one types, even with the aid of a spell checker or Microsoft Editor. The instantaneous reflex of seeing the blue squiggled line or the red squiggled line stops the process immediately, if just for a flicker of recognition that attention must be paid to the error at some point.

None of this happens quickly or produces a satisfying product quickly, and as such, flies in the face of the duplicitous cliché, "work smarter not harder." For many people, "smarter" has only one meaning: "faster." Media theorist Marshall McLuhan understood the power technology has over time, space, and pace, and wrote poetic warnings to us in texts like *Understanding Media: The Extensions of Man*, originally published in 1964. McLuhan explains how technology's most important impact on humans is on our perceptions—in most cases, that technology makes processes go faster, or even just adds an awareness of time to the proceedings. The most profound change, surely, is the light bulb, which altered our relationship to labor. Days that were once ruled by the rotation of the sun around the earth, where most laborious tasks had to be completed before sundown, were now upended by a false sun that did not set. The workday became infinite, or at least for as long as the bulb filament would last, and the electricity bill could be paid.

Consider the typewriter as the precursor of the personal computer and laptop. The typewriter works on two levels—accessibility-afforder and pace-accelerator, as an engine of speed and (some) uniformity. Famously, philosopher Friedrich Nietzsche found his work transformed when, for health reasons including the loss of his eyesight, he turned to Malling Hansen's writing ball to continue committing his ideas into permanence through writing. In his seminal tome *Gramophone, Film, Typewriter*, Friedrich Kittler (1999) devotes a section to the effects of the typewriter on Nietzsche's writing. He quotes Nietzsche thusly: "Our writing tools are also working on our thoughts," (200). Kittler (1999) notes that Nietzsche's writing "changed from arguments to aphorisms, from thoughts to puns, from rhetoric to telegram style [...] Malling Hansen's writing ball, with its operating difficulties, made Nietzsche into a laconic" (203). To a contemporary layperson, this sounds like the typewriter ushered us into the precursor of the Buzzfeed listicle. Here, we have this collision between disability and technology—Kittler notes that authors such as Mark Twain purchased typewriters to speed up their production, while Nietzsche purchased a typewriter to extend his ability to communicate his thoughts, having no way to effectively communicate with an air of permanence otherwise. At least, on his own.

There may have been other reasons for the change in Nietzsche's prose, including external frustrations that impeded his desire and ability to write in a fulsome manner. The reasons which led Nietzsche to change his thought preservation method may have impacted his philosophy even more than the tool he chose to remedy the situation, and all these factors may have woven together to create the emergent situation that altered Nietzsche's thoughts. When Nietzsche expresses, "Our writing tools are also working on our thoughts," we can remember to open our definition of tools to include all the matter, human and nonhuman, that can impact the creative process. Kittler invites us, repeatedly, to remember that the writing ball used by Nietzsche was created with inspiration from the deaf community. Kittler (1999) relates the history of Hans Rasmus Johann Malling Hansen, inventor of the *skrivekugle* (or writing ball), who was inspired by "the observation that his deaf-mute patients' sign language was faster than handwriting" to create a machine that "was meant to compensate for physiological deficiencies and to increase writing speed (which prompted the Nordic Telegraphy Co. to use "a number of writing balls for the transfer of incoming telegrams)" (202). Notice that the Nordic Telegraphy Company was using the writing balls to transfer information, not create it wholesale. The typewriter's early design was meant to be assistive rather than creative. We need to ask more questions about how one comes to use certain technologies, and how those technologies came into being, to assess how one element impacts the process rather than just the product or output.

A lack of clarity surrounding the network of tools that affect writers leads to "looking through a glass darkly," a phrase taken from 1 Corinthians 13:12 (*The Bible* 1997, 218), which reads, in its entirety, "For now we see through a glass, darkly; but then face to face: now I know in part; but then shall I know even as also I am known." When I think about the obfuscation surrounding the creation of generative AI and large language models (LLMs), I think about the image of a sight line being darkened or obscured. In so many ways, we have come to understand that fights for transparency and visibility are happening on innumerable fronts; it often feels as though when one researcher or reporter uncovers a bit of information, they have only peeled back one layer or dislodged one plank, the truth of which is often obscured further by ad hominem distractions. It is as if researchers of generative AI are looking through a plane of glass that is warped, discolored, and cracked in places, as we try to make sense of the bits and pieces of information either given forth by developers or uncovered by intrepid investigators. I do not use the Biblical phrase to suggest that we must wait until an afterlife for clarity—rather, I want to acknowledge that our perceptions of what generative AI developers and development entails is compromised, to highlight the people and the work being done to gain clarity, and to advocate for more transparency. The flawed glass in this metaphor is not inevitable, and thus, we can continue to press companies for essential information about their products and processes.

There are reasons why companies like OpenAI and Microsoft are interested in keeping this information vague and obscured from the public's prying eyes, but those reasons pale in comparison to the actual harm these companies do through their secrecy—in Chapter 3, I go into more detail regarding the obscurity that attends discussions about generative AI, especially regarding the data sets used and the environmental costs to creating and using these generative AI products. It seems a fool's errand to try to get these companies to spell out, in granular detail, even what their products do for consumers, let alone how they built their LLMs.

The answers to these questions matter to me because I believe we can gain some insight into the future of generative AI by looking at the conditions under which, and the way, these LLMs were built. Put another way: I think we learn more about Frankenstein's monster by looking at Victor Frankenstein, the world of the late eighteenth century, the history of the random body parts stolen by Frankenstein, the philosophies being taught at the University of Ingolstadt, information about the run of scarlet fever in Geneva, and so forth. To be sure, I am not being nosy for nosiness' sake. I am not trying to gain company secrets so that I may develop my own LLM. As I describe in Chapter 1, the genesis of this book project goes back to my research on the development of the steam-powered printing presses that form the blasting heartbeat of the periodical industry in nineteenth-century Britain; these presses, developed by Friedrick Koenig, were a vibrant assemblage of human and non-human materials. In that research, I was inspired by Bennett's (2010) theory of vibrant matter: all matter—human and non-human—is perpetually interacting with each other, influencing and being influenced, propelling and retracting, processing towards products (which, in turn, are part of a process to more products). These ideas offer a framework for how to see the disparate materials that are in conversation with each other and how we can learn more about an assemblage of matter by learning more about those disparate human and non-human bits. It is currently quite difficult to see clearly through the glass to tell what pieces and parts infuse their way into the assemblage of LLMs, and yet it is worth squinting and researching to learn more.

In terms of the British print industry of the nineteenth century, I was curious to learn if the process of acquiring the necessary raw materials to build the machines, make the ink, and print the paper, might echo some of the anxiety-ridden themes I was finding in the texts of *Lady Audley's Secret*, *The Moonstone*, and many of the Sherlock Holmes short stories printed in *The Strand Magazine*. The answer, after learning far more about esparto grass and iron mining than I would have ever imagined, was a resounding *yes.* If the process by which the dish is made is flawed, the food is going to taste a little funny. Today, people wisely point to the genesis of Facebook—as a platform where Mark Zuckerberg could take out his frustration over young women existing by mocking their appearances—might help explain how the website has rapidly devolved into a space for disinformation, data theft, propaganda, and the furthering of genocide. *If* Facebook ever had a *good* era, it was in the early 2000s, just after the doors were opened to non-college students, and people could connect with family and friends, especially those from whom they were physically distant. But it wasn't built for that, so that time was necessarily going to be short.

But even Facebook's successes and failures are not redounded to Zuckerberg's pathology alone. The knotty networks of people and things that make the world are a counterpoint to the myth of the "lone genius." First, let me note that I am not suggesting that preternaturally intelligent and talented people exist. I also believe in expertise; I do believe, however, that we should lean in more aggressively to the idea that no one person can be wholly knowledgeable in all areas—it is good and healthy for us all to divide the labor. It is good for me, for example, to focus on my areas of interest and attempt to master relevant skills, while I leave areas such as construction, physics, and political science to those who possess an interest and talent in those skill areas. No one needs me to assess whether a house has been built correctly, let me assure you. We should rely on others to share their knowledge and skills with us in a good faith manner.

The focus for me is the "lone" part of the myth, not the "genius" part. The "lone genius" figure of celebration rises out of the Enlightenment and is deified by the Romantic poets; the American obsession with "rugged individualism" and "bootstrap" ideology drills mythos into young minds as aggressively as it foregrounds concepts like Manifest Destiny and the "American Dream." Community and communal networks are seen as weak, enslaving, and feminine. Convincing people that they not only can do everything on their own, but that there is greater honor in solitary work has wreaked havoc on many aspects of our lives, not least of which is our concept of writing as meaningful work.

I have spent most of my life with a particular image of a "Writer" in mind—alone in a room, hunched over a keyboard or notebook for hours on end, subsisting on coffee (or stronger) to either fuel the production or to keep the demons at bay. It is easy to conjure images of Ernest Hemingway, Dylan Thomas, Dorothy Parker, or Stephen King, holed away in a musty room, crumpled loose leaf balled with smears of ink, sweat on their brows, torturing a manuscript out of their bodies, one paper cut at a time. One envisions Cenobites surrounding any would-be writer, offering them the chance to be tormented eternally for profit. Because that's what we are told it takes, in this fairytale—if you don't suffer alone, you cannot possibly create something of value. The triumph over suffering and self-abuse is the key to achievement and prosperity.

It does not take much thought to realize how unbelievably harmful these visions are. Isolation, substance abuse, monomania, and unrealistic expectations of what one can do on one's own may lead to some success, but they rarely come without costs. Famous writers have long been associated with issues of substance abuse, poor mental health outcomes, and often tragic interpersonal relationships. It is a wrong to suggest that people who experience such hardships can be considered icons whose behavior to be emulated, based solely on material achievements.

Most importantly, however, this vision of interminable self-reliance is patently false. There is no such thing as the "self-made man." Let us invoke poet John Donne (1990): "No man is an island" (344). With this assertion, I am not suggesting that writers do not work hard, or that they do not shoulder a significant part of the burden of the act of writing. Professional writers know that, unless you make time and embody some aspect of discipline, the work will not write itself (more's the pity!). The body and mind must be willing to think deeply, compose critically, and represent language in a more permanent way to write. Yet no one comes to the task of writing like Athena sprung from the head of Zeus. Writers have lived in communities, have gone to school, have read the works of other (often dead) authors, have consumed media, have eaten food grown by others, and have often been tended to by family or friends as they labored. Writers have lived and breathed the architecture and the natural environment that surrounds them, consciously or unconsciously. Even when they are holed up in their writing shacks, offices, or basements, they are touching some kind of technology that comes from somewhere else, be it paper, pencil or pen, or computers with their chips and wires. Read in such a way, there is no activity on earth more communal, philosophically, than writing, as the writer must call to mind all of their thoughts, memories, feelings, learnings, facts, perceptions, impressions (from every sense) gained through interactions with human and nonhuman entities, and attempt to put all of that input into words, in an order which will be both understandable and interesting to a reader.

We know that, in nearly all cases, the writing product is improved by sharing work with others for feedback. In classrooms, we use peer review exercises with the hope of not only improving each student's ability to edit and revise (and therefore, write), but also to strengthen each student's ability to be mindful of their writing, and to be able to have a dialogue about their writing. When we talk about writing as a craft, it is important to help novice writers learn to engage in discussions about their approaches and the approaches of others, which might offer new potent options.

Professional writers need editors, and the relationship between writers and editors is an important one. One thinks of editor Maxwell Perkins and his tumultuous relationships with Thomas Wolfe, F. Scott Fitzgerald, and Ernest Hemingway—so dynamic, in fact, that the relationships were dramatized in the 2016 film *Genius*. Note, not *Lone Genius*—these brilliant men were in no way alone on islands.

Given the Western concept of intellectual property, it is understandable how the obsession with solitary brilliance and the idea of "original thought" has taken over rational understanding of the interconnectedness of creativity. If we start examining closely the assemblage of information points in which we are enmeshed—if we see ourselves, as writers, as participants in a great collective, building on the information we take in, sharing our impressions with others—then we might find ourselves feeling in conflict with a notion that says we must be able to ruthlessly delineate what is yours and what is mine for reasons of capitalism. If I use too many quotations or sources, or even suggest that the work of others has clearly impacted my ideas, I experience a grim feeling that my product is less valuable.

I am not suggesting writers use work without crediting—I mean the opposite. As writers, we should be aiming for explicit transparency with respect to our information assemblages. That is, we should be offering greater context for how and why we arrive at our ideas, credit all the writers who have influenced us (not just the famous ones), and reestablish the communal nature of writing as opposed to reifying the myth of the "lone genius" artist. We can see ourselves and others as constantly building knowledge and see attribution via citation as demonstration of critical knowledge building infrastructures.

What does this look like in practice? Should we be looking back to the days of salons and writer collectives like the Bloomsbury Group or Algonquin Round Table? Perhaps, but only with the realization that those groups were exclusionary and largely remembered through mythology's haze. Who has time to indulge in long, liquor-soaked lunches, trading witticisms and sharpening one's craft? Recall Wordsworth's (1966) explanation of the craft of poetry: "[…] Poetry is the spontaneous overflow of powerful feelings: it takes its origin from emotion recollected in tranquility" (27). I want to not only focus on the concept of time, as I did briefly in Chapter 1, but also on the idea of "tranquility." The politics of slowing down impact all aspects of engaging with generative AI, but the idea of tranquility is, truly, tied to the capacity for creative production. This is not to say that tranquility is unimportant to reading and to teaching preparation, but I do want to tie an element of freedom from agitation and freedom from turmoil to the production of writing. Such a sentiment seems antithetical to everything we know about creativity—great works have always been produced in times of personal, political, or ecological strife. Put another way, great works have always been produced in response to times of personal, political, or ecological strife. In most cases, great writing has been produced when the writer has had some period of reflection and contemplation. In the best cases, we have a chance to be still, to be intentionally thoughtful, so that we may write ourselves into a greater understanding of the tribulation we have endured. This blessed repose has often only been afforded to some, but not all; we are certainly not living in a time of great affordance when it comes to opportunities to slow down, to rest, and to achieve a state of creative peace in which to compose. I will delve into this in greater detail in Chapter 5, which is focused on teaching, but we should all be talking with each other about ways to achieve these moments of relative peace where we can be critically creative.

Conclusion

We can use what we have learned from generative AI scraping and wasting to, instead, look for ways that generative AI tools might inspire us to be more supportive and more inclusive to all scholars. Bennett (2010) gives the fruitful example of the great North American blackout of 2003: "The electrical grid, by blacking out, lit up quite a lot: the shabby condition of the public-utilities infrastructure, the law-abidingness of New York City residents living in the dark […] and the element of unpredictability marking assemblages composed of intersecting and resonating elements" (36). The insertion of generative AI into our daily lives may feel like a blackout, pulling our attention from the topics that we'd rather be discussing, but what if we saw this moment as an opportunity, as a vibrant point of articulation: assemblage theory also, critically, offers language to describe "failure" in a way that does not suggest stoppage (for there never really is stoppage—matter continues to crash into each other). We can see the failures of generative AI as an opportunity to reassess what our most basic goals are, as a writing scholarly community. We can talk more, and talk more deeply, about why we write and what we do when challenges arise. We can talk about creating situations for ourselves and for others to experience deep writing, and we can take action to create such spaces that are seen as necessary.

References

Beddington, John, Cary L. Cooper, Usha Goswami, et al. 2008. "The Mental Wealth of Nations." *Nature* 455 (October).

Bennett, Jane. 2010. *Vibrant Matter: A Political Ecology of Things*. Duke University Press.

The Bible: Authorized King James Version with Apocrypha. 1997, edited by Robert Carroll and Stephen Prickett. Oxford University Press.

Borgstrom, Erica, Rachel Morris, Diana Wood, Simon Cohn, and Stephen Barclay. 2016. "Learning to Care: Medical Students' Reported Value and Evaluation of Palliative Care Teaching Involving Meeting Patients and Reflective Writing." *BMC Medical Education* 16 (1): 306. https://doi.org/10.1186/s12909-016-0827-6.

Donne, John. 1990. "From Devotions Upon Emergent Occasions." In *The Major Works*, edited by John Carey. Oxford University Press.

Doyle, Arthur Conan. 1892. "The Adventure of the Speckled Band." *Strand Magazine: An Illustrated Monthly* 3: 142–157.

Doyle, Arthur Conan. 1887. *A Study in Scarlet*. Beeton's Christmas Annual; 28th Season. London; Ward Lock & Co.

Emig, Janet. 1977. "Writing as a Mode of Learning." *College Composition and Communication* 28 (2): 122–28.

Fairie, Paul. [@paulisci.bsky.social]. (2025, March 31). A Brief History of Kids Today Are Lazy. View: https://bsky.app/profile/paulisci.bsky.social/post/3llpevyi3f22n. [Post]. Bluesky.

Finkenstaedt-Quinn, Solaire A., Michael Petterson, Anne Gere, and Ginger Shultz. 2021. "Praxis of Writing-to-Learn: A Model for the Design and Propagation of Writing-to-Learn in STEM." *Journal of Chemical Education* 98 (5): 1548–1555. https://doi.org/10.1021/acs.jchemed.0c01482.

Gonzalez, Emily, Henley Cox and Sammy Smart, hosts. 2024. Too Scary, Didn't Watch. "Bone Tomahawk." September 25. Podcast, 1 hour, 24 min., 46 sec. https://headgum.com/too-scary-didnt-watch/bone-tomahawk.

Kittler, Friedrich. 1999. *Gramophone, Film, Typewriter*. Translated by Geoffrey Winthrop-Young and Michael Wutz. Stanford University Press.

McLuhan, Marshall. 2013. *Understanding Media: The Extensions of Man*, edited by W. Terrance Gordon. Ginko Press.

Ray, Karen, Kerry Dally, Kim Colyvas, and Alison E. Lane. 2021. "The Effects of a Whole-Class Kindergarten Handwriting Intervention on Early Reading Skills." *Reading Research Quarterly* 56 (S1). https://doi.org/10.1002/rrq.395.

Wordsworth, William. 1966. "Preface to Lyrical Ballads, with Other Poems." In *Literary Criticism of William Wordsworth*, edited by Paul M. Zall. University of Nebraska Press.

Zacharopoulos, George, Francesco Sella, and Roi Cohen Kadosh. 2021. "The Impact of a Lack of Mathematical Education on Brain Development and Future Attainment." *Proceedings of the National Academy of Sciences* 118 (24): e2013155118. https://doi.org/10.1073/pnas.2013155118.

CHAPTER 3

Making Bricks Without Clay: Generative AI and Reading

Abstract Reading requires a level of trust that the author is acting in good faith, yet generative AI is untrustworthy. This chapter outlines how difficult, yet critical, it is for us to try to "read" generative AI so that we can more clearly interpret what affect is can and does have on the humanities and on our daily lives, including our ability to acquire and maintain literacy and deep reading skills.

Keywords Reading · Generative AI · Literacy

Introduction

In "The Adventure of the Copper Beeches," Sherlock Holmes and Dr. John Watson are visited by a young woman, Miss Violet Hunter, who is concerned about accepting a to-good-to-be-true offer of employment from wealthy eccentrics. At his bidding, she tells Holmes the details of her story—the oddities, the over-payment for a governess with few talents—and yet she says, "[…] my mind is made up that I will accept [the position of governess]. I thought, however, that before taking the final step, I should like to submit the whole matter to your consideration" (Doyle 1892, 617). Holmes replies that if her mind is made up, that is the end of discussion. She presses him, and he underscores that, while he cannot

D. J. Gavin, *Generative AI and the Future of the Humanities*,
https://doi.org/10.1007/978-3-032-06534-6_3

tell her specifically what dangers lay ahead, "I confess that it is not the situation which I should like to see a sister of mine apply for" (Doyle 1892, 617). This answer does not satisfy her, as she declares, "'But the money, Mr. Holmes, the money!'" (Doyle 1892, 617). When she has Holmes' assurance that he will spring into action if she finds herself in distress and calls for him, she expresses contentment and sets off to cut her hair and travel to the Copper Beeches.

For days after Miss Hunter departs, Watson observes Holmes in a state of frustrated thought. When questioned, Watson notes that Holmes erupts: "'Data! data! data!' he cried impatiently. 'I can't make bricks without clay.' And yet he would always wind up by muttering that no sister of his should ever have accepted such a situation" (Doyle 1892, 618). Often, this quotation about data is taken out of the narrative context of the story and used, along with other quotes from other Sherlock Holmes stories about the need for data, to point to a character trait and talent of the Great Detective. I will explore that point later, but first, I want to return to the narrative context and its association with generative AI.

In the course of telling her tale, Violet discloses many moments that shock or concern her—her would-be employer proposes to pay her an absurd sum of money to care for only one child, on the condition that she wear a particular dress and cut off her beautiful auburn hair. When she declines his initial offer, Mr. Rucastle presses the employment agency to give him Violet's address, and he writes a detailed and overbearing telegram to her, proposing even more money. She chooses to confide all of this to Holmes, and by extension, Watson, and is dismayed at Holmes' concern for her safety. Her preoccupation is with the enormous sum of money, and it is difficult to blame her. As we learn so painfully from Jane Austen and Charlotte Brontë, among others, the lives of governesses were not to be admired. Violet sees an opportunity here to sacrifice a core element of her beauty and her safety for the chance to secure a handsome amount of money that may give her more opportunities to escape from a life of servitude. She just wants Holmes to tell her that he will be there when everything goes to hell in a handbasket. Which everyone seems to agree will likely happen.

I believe many people in and around the conversations about generative AI would empathize with Sherlock Holmes in this situation. First, I think people who have been at the fore of warning about the dangers surrounding LLMs, such as Emily M. Bender, Timnit Gebru, Angelina

McMillan-Major, and Margaret Mitchell among many others, would appreciate Holmes' declaration that no sister of his would be taking this governess position. Based on all the data we have at hand, the sum of its parts points towards knowable cons, and only the vaguest of pros.

Reading Generative AI

What do we know about generative AI? What, then, can we *read* right now, with respect to generative AI? What steps can we take towards an AI literacy that is primarily concerned with what a thing does, how has it been made, and who are the makers? Most overviews of generative AI make it clear that this technology is not new, per se. Harvard University Information Technology sums it up nicely: "Generative AI is a type of artificial intelligence that can learn from and mimic large amounts of data to create content such as text, images, music, videos, code, and more, based on inputs or prompts" (Generative Artificial Intelligence (AI) 2025). Cornell University's Center for Teaching Innovation notes that LLMs are one popular type of model, and that they "typically consist of millions or billions of parameters that are 'trained' on massive amounts of text data" (*Generative Artificial Intelligence | Center for Teaching Innovation* 2025). Note that Cornell University puts the term "trained" in quotation marks—this is a good strategy, one I am trying to adopt completely in my practice. We have been conditioned to use terms that apply only to sentient beings in relation to the system output of programs. Cornell further suggests that "LLMs can also learn from their own outputs and are likely to improve over time"—I would prefer to put "learn" in quotation marks here too (*Generative Artificial Intelligence | Center for Teaching Innovation* 2025). Importantly, Cornell concedes that LLMs cannot offer intelligent context (that is, they have no capacity for understanding); "[r]ather, LLMs generate new content based on patterns in existing content, and build text by predicting most likely words" (*Generative Artificial Intelligence | Center for Teaching Innovation* 2025).

We have, in general, allowed technology developers to get away pretending it's all a bit *hocus pocus*. Instead of telling consumers, "Pay no attention to the man behind the curtain!" developers have been not only allowed but encouraged to say, "I don't see anything and you don't either." Hype and misdirection have led to what Ed Zitron calls "The Rot Economy," but first, it leads to illiteracy by creating a situation in which consumers cannot read either the products they are being sold or the companies doing the selling. How have we ended up in a situation where consumers are being told they should be awestruck by products they cannot see or understand?

Returning to "The Adventure of the Copper Beeches": when Holmes hears Violet's tale, he understands that the pieces do not add up; he remarks, "'Well, yes, of course the pay is good—too good. That is what makes me uneasy. Why should they give you £120 a year, when they could have their pick for £40? There must be some strong reason behind'" (Doyle 1892, 617). Neither Holmes nor Violet Hunter can perceive exactly what will happen if she becomes the governess at the Copper Beeches, but Holmes rightly assesses that the proposed payoff does not match the vagaries surrounding the job description. This, to me, reflects the grandiose over-promising committed by leading developers. When something seems too good to be true, it probably is.

One can conjure up some of the incredible promises made by generative AI developers—AI will solve climate change, eliminate biases that come from human decision-making, and, above all, everyone will have so much time saved through automation and generation that we will all be free to do … *things*. Important things, things that require a higher level of human achievement. I will explore more about the relationship between labor and rest in concert with generative AI promises in Chapter 4, but it is important to note here that we are being promised a utopia, and yet, when we ask, "How are these miracles possible?" developers seem to be as bewildered as we are. It is insufficient for companies to still throw their hands up and say, "It's all just a mystery, isn't it?" and cling to the black box argument.

First, let us take up the miracles promised. I have a vague idea in my head about what generative AI can do, but it does become quite difficult to find concrete examples from the hype merchants. Ed Zitron, in an episode of his podcast *Better Offline*, titled, "Monologue: The Super Bowl Showed That Generative AI is Washed," describes the *seemingly* evocative ads run by Google and OpenAI during the 2025 Super Bowl broadcast. These ads are incredibly expensive and promise to command a record number of eyes (as the Super Bowl is one of the most-watched televised events in the United States). Zitron summarizes the two ads: first up is Google, which is an ad for both Google's Pixel 9 and Gemini Live, Google's generative AI product that will come preloaded on the smartphone. Open AI's commercial, titled "The Intelligence Age," "showed a dot matrix history of time involving men throwing spears, people riding horses […] A full forty seconds into this one-minute long commercial, we start hearing prompts" (Zitron 2025, at 2:30–3:00). Neither ad actually shows generative AI "doing" something or producing something useful. At one point, the Google commercial shows the older man using Google Search, not Gemini. Gemini provides milquetoast answers to unheard prompts, such as "try rephrasing your answer to sound more confident" (Zitron 2025, at 2:07). OpenAI's ad features ChatGPT "helping" a person practice negotiating for a raise, which Zitron argues "feels like more of a cruel joke" as AI is poised to "actually [wreck] the labor market as they wanted to" (Zitron 2025, at 4:17).

Zitron does his best debunking, however, when he takes apart Salesforce's ad, featuring actor Matthew McConaughey running through Heathrow airport, lamenting that he cannot find his gate due to his failure to use Salesforce's AI agent, Agent Force. If viewed in a vacuum, the ad makes it seem like using Agent Force is a crucial step for a would-be traveler attempting to navigate massive airports like Heathrow—Salesforce sounds powerful and life-improving, and the very sort of ap that I should be downloading onto my smartphone right now. A cursory look in the app store does not turn up anything named "Salesforce" that seems relevant to travel, however. Thankfully Zitron took his rightful skepticism and researched how Heathrow and Salesforce have teamed up to create this incredible user experience; he discovered that Heathrow has been using Salesforce's Einstein chatbot to manage customer service inquiries to slightly increase responsiveness. There is no opportunity for a traveler to make use of "Agent Force," even if Heathrow was integrating some kind of AI agent. Zitron makes the searing point, "They [Salesforce] can't do an ad that says, hey, do you want a slightly more powerful chatbot that costs a great deal of money? So, they have to make this kind of incongruent ad that lies about their product without ever really saying what it does" (Zitron 2025, at 7:28–7:50). Zitron further assails the developers, saying, "Vague and blatant lies that barely masked the contempt that these companies have for customers, so much contempt that they can't even bother to give them a real reason to use it" (Zitron 2025, at 7:52–8:10). I appreciate how Zitron is able to read straight through the gauzy platitudes offered by these commercials to zero in on the absolute nothingness they offer consumers. We must reckon with the idea that companies like Google and OpenAI are not in the business of selling a product that produces. They are selling a level of acceptance rather than understanding, shifting the Overton Window, on what the consumer will tolerate and ultimately celebrate.

There are efforts to require more transparency, as efficiently cataloged on White & Case's *AI Watch: Global Regulatory Tracker*: in February 2024, the United Kingdom's government published *A Pro-Innovation Approach to AI Regulation—Government Response to Consultation*, in which they highlight "Appropriate transparency and explainability" as one of the five principles for existing regulators. On the website gov.uk, a page titled "Best Practice AI: Developing an explainability statement for an AI-enabled medical symptom checker," offers an explanation and an example of what an "explainability statement" would look like for a company preparing to integrate AI into their processes. In the United States, at this moment in early 2025, there are no comprehensive federal laws or regulations that pertain to AI, though there are some 100-plus bills working their way through the US Congress ("AI Watch" 2025). In October 2022, the White House Office of Science and Technology Policy (OSTP) published "Blueprint for an AI Bill of Rights," which offered guidelines for equitable use of and access to AI. On May 17, 2024, Colorado passed the Colorado AI Act, the first comprehensive US AI legislation at the state level. That same month, Utah passed the Utah Artificial Intelligence Policy Act, which requires anyone who used generative AI in communications to disclose such use with their consumers. In September 2024, California enacted various AI bills, including Assembly Bill 2013 (AB 2013), set to take effect in 2026, which will require a high level of transparency that should, in theory, help dismantle the "black box" problem.

Efforts at forcing transparency have not always created the most effective outcomes. In January 2021, HireVue, a well-known AI-powered hiring platform employed by Mercedes-Benz, KraftHeinz, and General Mills among others, announced that it would cease using the facial analysis component of its hiring services. Concerns had been raised surrounding the use of AI in hiring, and specifically, concerns about the use of facial recognition software were highlighted: the Institute of Electrical and Electronics Engineers (IEEE) Public Safety Technology Initiative (2025) notes that current facial recognition systems have low accuracy rates when examining the faces of women and people of color, as "[…]bias can stem from various sources, including underrepresentation in training data, algorithmic design choices, and even the underlying physics of how different skin tones interact with camera sensors." HireVue suggested that its system of predictive transcription led to greater accuracies than its facial analysis system—which, to be clear, entailed an algorithm assigning meaning to certain facial expressions and movements during a recorded job interview with an AI chatbot—and thus they dumped the facial analysis portion (Maurer 2021).

A press release, dated March 31, 2022, promotes HireVue's AI Explainability Statement, which they note is "[a]n HR industry first." According to the company's Explainability Statement, HireVue uses AI to transcribe spoken words to text (presumably, the interviewee's responses to questions posed by the AI interviewer), interpreting that text, and scoring the text "based on expert human rater evaluations of answers to similar competency-based interview questions" (HireVue Explainability Statement). The Explainability Statement notes that HireVue's AI only evaluates text, and does not review or assess the video or audio portions of the interview; they specify, "[...] [W]e do not assess a candidate's facial expressions, body language, their background and surroundings, or tone-of-voice" (HireVue Explainability Statement). They clarify, "Before completing a HireVue AI-scored assessment, applicants review an AI consent statement and have the option to opt in or out of the use of AI in evaluating their responses" (HireVue Explainability Statement). The HireVue website includes a document of tips specifically for neurodiverse candidates, which includes information about declining a HireVue-run interview and requesting accommodations for their neurodiversity. According to the tips document, "The Company may offer you a formal face-to-face interview or an alternate method of assessment" and HireVue offers some ideas regarding concerns over disclosing a diagnosis (HireVue Explainability Statement). They note, "[...] [O]pting out of AI evaluation will not exclude a candidate from participating [in] the hiring process" (HireVue Explainability Statement). If a person declines to go through the AI evaluation process, "[...] recruiters manually review and rate these candidates' interview responses based on the same behaviorally anchored rating scales describing low, medium, and high performance on the relevant competency(ies)" (HireVue Explainability Statement).

Matt Scherer (2022) notes that while HireVue's Explainability Statement offers some useful information, it elides important information and offers glimpses into failures. He does praise the readability of the documents and some helpful disclosures. However, as he writes under "The Bad: Concerning Disclosures," "Some disclosed 'competencies' that

HireVue assesses pose a risk of discrimination to disabled workers." Moreover, he writes, "Given that HireVue delivers its assessments through its integrated 'end-to-end hiring platform,' it is not clear if or how employers could offer any other accommodations to disabled workers, aside from having them assessed by completely different means" (Scherer 2022). And he argues that HireVue remains vague on many other details, including kicking the can of responsibility to employers with respect to EU/UK data regulations and a dearth of information regarding how game-based assessments are made.

Is HireVue's Explainability Statement a step in the right direction? Absolutely! Especially as it helps make the case why this company is still lacking. If I were the head of a Human Resources department, I would be more inclined to work with a company that is taking steps towards transparency than those who cling, desperately, to the black box of hype potential. Scherer's assessment, though, points out that transparency is not a goal unto itself. The high potential for discrimination against those with disabilities should be a non-starter in terms of industry standards and should compel HireVue to drastically rethink its procedures. A document without internal review and revision is insufficient, but it seems like a necessary first step towards the sort of radical readability we require.

Environmental Costs

One of the bigger illegibility behemoths is the energy and environmental costs of generative AI. In their groundbreaking 2021 article, "On the Dangers of Stochastic Parrots: Can Language Models Be Too Big?", authors Bender et al. (2021) point to the research of Strubell et al. (2019), who measured model training and development costs in terms of financial impact and carbon dioxide emissions. They found that training a Transformer model with neural architecture search generated approximately 56.8 times more carbon dioxide than an average human generates per year. Bender et al. (2021) summarize their findings thusly: "Training a single BERT base model (without hyperparameter tuning) on GPUs was estimated to require as much energy as a trans-American flight" (612). That translates into a meaningful carbon footprint.

Next, consider the scale—Strubell et al. (2019) were looking at the impact of one model, but those models are housed *en masse* in data centers which are rarely visible in our daily comings and goings. From one point of view, even when taken collectively, the energy consumption of models is far less than other energy expenditures. In a 2024 report for The International Energy Agency (IEA), Spenser and Singh note that data centers currently account for approximately 1 percent of global electricity consumption, which is roughly half of the energy consumed by regular household appliance usage. Take the January 2025 Substack post by Andy Masley, director of Effective Altruism DC, titled "Using ChatGPT is Not Bad for The Environment," where he makes the case that one person's use of ChatGPT is far less impactful than their use of Spotify or video-streaming services. He argues that worrying about the energy consumption of ChatGPT is "wasted time that you could spend on the serious problems of climate change instead" (Masley 2025). In fact, he casts this distraction as nefarious when he writes, "[I]f you're worried at all about your own use of AI contributing to climate change, you have been tricked into constructing monsters in your head and you need to snap out of it" (Masley 2025). Masley makes a keen point that people are unaware of how much energy and water they are consuming daily, though he gets over his skis when he argues that we should continue apace with energy guzzlers like Spotify. He writes, "The energy involved in streaming a Spotify song is much much less than the energy required to physically produce and distribute music CDs, cassettes, and records" (Masley 2025). I will save a lengthier argument regarding labor for Chapter 4, but suffice it to say that the irony is not lost on me that Masley is skimming right over one of the key arguments against Spotify—namely cheating artists out of fair compensation and eliding their agency as the talent producers—and for that reason, presumably we should be considering a return to CDs, cassettes, and records.

I should also note here that many people claim generative AI will be invaluable in the fight against climate change and environmental degradation. For example, according to Julie Sweet (2024), Chair and Chief Executive Officer of Accenture, "As energy businesses work to reach their sustainability goals, reinvent their enterprises and succeed in the energy transition to net zero, they have a powerful new ally: generative AI" (36). Sweet gives a few examples of how generative AI is being used now, which essentially boil down to using LLMs as chatbots, and proposes that generative AI will be harnessed by companies to save time and create efficiencies. Microsoft reports a partnership with researchers at the Massachusetts Institute of Technology (MIT) and University of California, Berkeley (UC Berkeley) to use generative machine learning models to investigate and generate materials that could be useful for carbon capture, a three-step process where the carbon that is naturally produced during industrial processes is isolated, transported, and buried underground in rock formations (Smith & Nakagawa 2023).

There is a dearth of specific examples of how generative AI will be helpful—largely, it amounts to generative AI analyzing data to find patterns of waste and looking for inefficiencies, which presumably could be applied by companies to their pollution-heavy processes.

Before we delve into individual usage, let me go back to data centers and the proliferation of them. According to McKinsey & Company, the United States presently accounts for about 40 percent of the global data center market (Bangalore et al. 2023). Based on data centers listed by Cloudscene (an Australian telecommunications service provider), Statista reported 5381 as of March 2024, with Germany in second place with 521 data centers. The fact that these centers currently account for 1 percent of energy consumption does not reflect the current obsession with growth. As Spenser and Singh (2024) write, if companies continue to buy into the expectations for AI, there will be a dramatic rise in the number, and notably, the size, of data centers. They suggest that some impact will be mitigated by developers making improvements in both hardware and software efficiencies, but that progress will only go so far to compensate for unchecked demand (if the current fever continues unabated); they anticipate increasing demands for electricity as data centers multiply up to the year 2030 (Spenser & Singh 2024).

A critical problem with this type of growth is the unanticipated hardships in local communities. As a person born and raised in New Orleans, with most of my family still in the area, I have been monitoring the development of the following story: in December 2024, Meta announced it will build a $10 billion artificial intelligence data center in northeast Louisiana, to be completed by 2030. What may seem like a boon to impoverished areas of Louisiana reads like the start of any number of "broken promise" stories. First, Meta is suggesting that the data center will support 500 or more direct new jobs in Richland Parish, but for a state that is ranked last or near the bottom in most metrics, it is hard to imagine that the workforce will not be imported, and that will bring challenges of its own. Grow NELA President and CEO Rob Cleveland seems to acknowledge that Meta is not coming to northeast Louisiana for the talent when he says, "Meta chose northeast Louisiana because of the availability of reliable, low-cost energy; access to flat, developable land and a business-friendly environment led by Governor Landry" ("Meta

Selects Northeast Louisiana" 2024). Of the many concerns with this statement, the one that jumps out the most is "reliable, low-cost energy," when, according to the *Louisiana Illuminator's* Wesley Muller (2025), Louisiana residents pay higher electricity bills than the national average based on one of the least reliable electric grids in the country, courtesy of Entergy Louisiana, the region's energy company. Muller's reporting, based on a report from Louisiana Legislative Auditor's Office titled "Louisiana's Electric Profile," notes that Louisiana residents use the most electricity per capita in the nation, even ahead of Alaska, and that electricity is generated primarily through gas and other fossil fuels, which portends an unsustainable future. It is, therefore, rich, to read from the Louisiana Economic Development's press release from December 2024, which states, "To power the data center, which at its largest point extends more than one mile from front to back, Entergy will add clean, efficient power plants to its system to meet growing power demands, including from the data center" ("Meta Selects Northeast Louisiana" 2024). And I am not certain I feel confident in Meta's "pledge" to "match its electricity use with 100% clean and renewable energy and will be working with Entergy to bring at least 1500 MW of new renewable energy to the grid through its Geaux Zero program" ("Meta Selects Northeast Louisiana" 2024).

Why do I worry so? As Spenser and Singh (2024) argue, "The growth of data centres could therefore lead to considerable strain on local power networks, exacerbated by the huge mismatch between rapid data centre construction times and the often sluggish pace of expanding and strengthening grids and generation capacity." One can look at the situation unfolding in Ireland currently for a glimpse inside the data center crystal ball. In most respects, Ireland was the model for recovery after the 2008 financial crisis, kicking off a tech-driven growth spurt dubbed "The Celtic Tiger" boom at the turn of the twenty-first century. More recently, Dublin has become the hot spot for companies looking to build their data centers for many reasons, but not least of which because Ireland tends to have a cooler climate for most of the year, which helps naturally cool off these burning centers without adding the burden of increased water usage in the cooling process (O'Brien 2024). What seemed like a brilliant move to add a small element of environmental care to the process—that is, for companies to make strategic choices about where they build centers to lower the water usage—has not borne out positive solutions.

It turns out that, even if the cooling process is more environmentally friendly, the resulting strain on the local grids becomes too much too fast. In Ireland's case, the national grid operator has halted new data center construction near Dublin until 2029, for fears of rolling blackouts that would rock the financial center of the country and the residents of the capital city. As O'Brien (2024) reports, "These huge buildings and their powerful computers last year consumed 21% of the nation's electricity, according to official records. No other country has reported a higher burden to the International Energy Agency."

It just doesn't seem to add up, does it? We're told, on one hand, that generative AI doesn't use *that* much energy, and that if we are really worried about the environment, we would focus our energies on other, larger scale but also not-super-useful energy-guzzlers, since *those* guzzlers are fun and therefore not *too* bad. Perhaps it's important to note, here, that Masley, like some "luminaries" in Silicon Valley, is a proponent of "effective altruism," a twenty-first century philosophical and social movement that advocates using reason and logic to make choices about who will be helped and how they will be helped based on the perception of greatest need. This sounds like a responsible approach to philanthropy and the world in general when considering the limited funds most of us possess—for example, I may consider donating to a national organization that can include my paltry sum with a much larger pool of money in a high-interest bearing account, with the knowledge that the national organization will have the resources to multiply my money and help more people. Seems lovely. What effective altruism and its offspring, longtermism, suggest, however, is a way to think of the hardships of today as being less important than an overarching bright future for some. In the case of generative AI, it is about putting a lot of faith in the magical promises—those black box mysteries we've been sold on—that are going to make some people a great deal of money now, and even more people (future people, many not even a glimmer in their mother's eye yet) wildly happy and successful in a glorious and unpromised future. Possibly I lack imagination, but I believe that, based on what I can read now, and what I can study from the past, we have very little reason to be hopeful of that bright horizon as it stands today at the feet of Sam Altman, co-founder and chief executive officer of OpenAI. From what I am reading, we should not be throwing the baby out with the bathwater and climbing over drowning children to save our metaphorical fancy suits for the generative AI dinner parties of the future (forgive my oblique reference to Peter

Singer's (1997) "drowning child" analogy). Indeed, as Ana Balashova (2024) offers, "But here's another brain teaser: as we embrace generative AI, are we truly safeguarding our planet, or are we merely witnessing a grand illusion where environmental debts are conveniently erased with the stroke of tech money?" It seems that Silicon Valley's response to charges of environmental impact is to buy their way out of scrutiny, often through purchasing carbon credits. In January 2025, the *Financial Times* reported Microsoft entered into a deal with Re.green, a Brazilian start-up that plants native tree species in Brazil's Amazon and Atlantic forests, where Microsoft will purchase 3.5 million dollars of carbon credits over the next 25 years (Bryan 2025). The planted trees are meant to balance out the overwhelming greenhouse gas emissions produced by Microsoft, which, according to their *2024 Environmental Sustainability Report*, has surged 30.9 percent since 2020 (5). Scope 3, which represents 96 percent of Microsoft's greenhouse gas emissions, includes the expansion of data centers meant to power the ascendancy of generative AI. Truly, Microsoft is committed to buying their way out of some of this trouble; as they note in their white paper, "A New Approach for Scope 3 Emissions Transparency," (2021) the company is committed to reducing their energy consumption and "has maintained 100 percent renewable electricity (achieved partially through power purchase agreements and renewable energy certificates)" (6).

I appreciate Balashova's energy when she writes, "Generative AI is the new rock star of the tech world. But it's shredding energy resources like there's no tomorrow. This isn't your grandma's calculator's AI. This is AI on steroids [...]" (Balashova 2024). She deftly parses how the different ways one might use ChatGPT, for example, matters profoundly: "While a single GPT query might be more energy-intensive than a Google search, the sheer volume of Google searches could potentially make its overall energy consumption significantly higher" (Balashova 2024). If consumer behavior switched from using Google Search to chatbots for the sort of mundane, routine searching one does multiple times daily (for which we coined the term "Googling,"), that kind of usage would certainly result in visible energy costs. In some ways, that could represent the most dangerous type of usage.

Let us imagine that everyone sat down at their computers, or unlocked their smartphones, and went right to ChatGPT, in place of opening Google, when looking up information. Kate Saenko (2023) argues that this would have serious energy costs as usage would add up over time and further suggests that "AI assistants have many more uses than just search, such as writing documents, solving math problems and creating marketing campaigns." Maybe, if we are acculturated to using generative AI for one use, especially the seemingly mundane, we will be more inclined to use generative AI for more mediocre uses? That's part of the confusion, right? At present, generative AI impacts the environment less than other activities. Yet, we are being told that generative AI will be omnipresent in our lives *soon*, doing all the sort of thinking tasks that we don't want to do, and don't want to make time to do. Generative AI is not about to do any of the things that the Super Bowl ads suggest, nor is it able to destroy the global community, as Eisikovits (2023) argues: "The technology is far from being able to decide on and then plan out the goals and subordinate goals necessary for shutting down traffic in order to get you a seat in a restaurant, or blowing up a car factory in order to satisfy your itch for paper clips." It's everything and nothing, all at once.

At the end of the day, the arguments over the impact of generative AI on the environment curdle down into what economists call Jevons' Paradox. Nineteenth-century economist William Stanley Jevons was invested in British dominance and was concerned that the rising cost of coal was a threat to Britain's geopolitical standing. He noted the relationship between access and use based on efficiency. Technology in the nineteenth century made it so that machines need less coal to work than they needed previously. Thus, one would imagine that if every machine in Britain needed less coal per blast session, less coal would be consumed. However, that was not the case: demand for coal increased, thus the paradox. Jevons (1895) writes, "If the quantity of coal used in a blast-furnace, for instance, be diminished in comparison with the yield, the profits of the trade will increase, new capital will be attracted, the price of pig-iron will fall, but the demand for it increase; and eventually the greater number of furnaces will more than make up for the diminished consumption of each." (104–105). Jevons was not concerned with the environmental cost of coal burning, but his paradox is helpful for us today. Clark and Foster (2001) put the paradox in modern terms: "technology by itself (given certain patterns of production and accumulation) offers no way out of our environmental dilemmas, which increase with the scale of the economy" (97). Put another way: people often expect that when technology brings efficiency to a process, there will ultimately be a reduction in consumption, *a la*, "Chatbots are less energy expensive than Spotify, so definitely keep using Chatbots because you will be consuming less energy." Unfortunately, as Jevons observed and we continue to learn over and over again, if you make something efficient and accessible, demand will increase, and your gains in efficiency will be lost. As Luccioni et al. (2025) argue, "These second-order effects challenge the presumption that purely technical optimizations alone will deliver sufficient climate benefits," as the production of efficient software may inspire developers to create new AI usages, which will in turn increase the demand for more hardware upgrades.

Abuses

The dramatic change we see with the emergence of OpenAI's ChatGPT on the landscape in the fall of 2022 is primarily due to the size and scale of the amount of training data that OpenAI used to create ChatGPT. Bender et al. (2021) expound upon the risks involved with sloppy upscaling that leads to biased output, environmental costs, and more. I will return to this article throughout this book; for this chapter, I would like to focus on Bender et al.'s (2021) arguments regarding the dangers of ginormous, filthy data sets and making meaning where none should even be attempted. They write of "[...] the tendency of training data ingested from the Internet to encode hegemonic worldviews, the tendency of LMs to amplify biases and other issues in the training data, and the tendency of researchers and other people to mistake LM-driven performance gains for actual natural language understanding — present real-world risks of harm, as these technologies are deployed" (616). LLMs, they describe, are built from "large, uncurated, Internet-based datasets [that] encode the dominant/hegemonic view, which further harms people at the margins" (613). Bender et al. (2021) offer a salient example: "[...] GPT-2's training data is sourced by scraping outbound links from Reddit, and Pew Internet Research's 2016 survey reveals 67% of Reddit users in the United States are men, and 64% between ages 18 and 29. Similarly, recent surveys of Wikipedians find that only 8.8–15% are women or girls" (613). The threat is profound: "In accepting large amounts of web text as 'representative' of 'all' of humanity we risk perpetuating dominant viewpoints, increasing power imbalances, and further reifying inequality" (614). Bender et al. (2021) point to one challenge to breaking down the hegemony: "Given the compute costs alone of training large LMs, it likely isn't feasible for even large corporations to fully retrain them frequently enough to keep up with the kind of language change discussed here" (614).

Questions remain, of course: how exactly does the process of putting words in order work? Where are those words (and images) coming from? What is in the data set, and how was the data obtained? And, importantly, how was the data set vetted?

Early iterations of chatbots had a propensity to veer into racist, misogynist, and violent language when used by the public. In March 2016, Microsoft released a chatbot called "Tay," and created a Twitter handle for the bot, encouraging fellow Twitter users to interact with the account so "it would tweet back, learning as it went from other users' posts" (Kraft 2016). "Tay," which presented as a young woman (many have done incredible research on the phenomenon of AI having feminine presentations and the fallout from that; see Costa (2018), Elder (2022), and Woods (2018)), lasted all of a day, as the bot began to respond with vile racist and abusive language, such as "Hitler was right I hate the jews" and "Ted Cruz is the Cuban Hitler." One might rightly ask, how could a chatbot go so wrong so quickly, and why was this product released to the public if this result was a possibility? The larger the dataset, the better the chatbot, and thus companies deploy web crawlers to scrape up as much data as possible, irrespective of copyright and legality, it seems. For BBC Science Focus, Alex Hughes reports, "The model was trained using text databases from the internet. This included a whopping 570 GB of data obtained from books, web texts, Wikipedia, articles and other pieces of writing on the internet." If you have ever used the Internet for any length of time, you have probably noticed that humans put the content onto it, and if humans are behind something, depravity will always find a way to emerge. We only need to remember the early days of Reddit, with forums such as "r/jailbait" and "r/beatingwomen," before Reddit began banning forums with explicitly racist, misogynist, bigoted, violent, and sexually abusive content.

Of course, Reddit does not even represent the worst content on the internet, and OpenAI—the company behind ChatGPT—has never been transparent about how they have created (and continue to develop) the data sets for the LLM. However, a lawsuit filed in 2023 alleges that OpenAI scraped significant amounts of data from social media posts, including Reddit and websites linked to Reddit posts (Dean 2023). The lawsuit and reporting give us a pretty good idea of what has been amassed. Authors Sarah Silverman, Paul Tremblay, and others have filed lawsuits in the United States over copyright infringement in California in 2023; the Silverman/Tremblay lawsuit has been partially dismissed (David 2024).

Later in 2023, the Authors Guild and 17 fiction heavy weights like John Grisham, George R.R. Martin, and Jodi Picoult filed the lawsuit against OpenAI in the Southern District of New York (David 2023). A group of authors filed a class action lawsuit against Anthropic for unauthorized use of their books for training models (Roth 2024). OpenAI has been clear that they do not believe scraping text off the internet should constitute a copyright violation—they argue that the pirated books (remember, the authors did not consent to have their ebooks included in data scraping adventures; current authors are being asked to surrender those rights, a topic I will discuss further in Chapter 4) are data to be rightfully mined for LLMs.

OpenAI goes so far as to make it clear that they cannot operate *without* scraping up copyrighted material. In response to the 2025 White House Office of Science and Technology (OSTP) appeal for public comment on a future US AI Action Plan, OpenAI wrote, "If the PRC's developers have unfettered access to data and American companies are left without fair use access, the race for AI is effectively over" (Lehane 2025, 10). OpenAI's submission is a document full of threats, but this one in particular chills me, and it seems to be such full-on naked jingoism as a ploy to bully creators into compliance.

Even more concerning are the lengths to which OpenAI and other companies are willing to go to clean up the data. Billy Perrigo's harrowing January 2023 article for *Time* titled, "OpenAI Used Kenyan Workers on Less Than $2 Per Hour to Make ChatGPT Less Toxic," details the unethical use of human labor to develop a tagging detector system. Perrigo explains how GPT-3 (ChatGPT's predecessor) was quick to delve into racist, violent, and abusive language, and OpenAI modeled their solution for this problem off Facebook's poorly realized solution to their violent content problem: they had to create a detector system based off tags, so their gigantic database could be scrubbed before future chatbots were released. To create those tagging systems, OpenAI needed human operators to sift through tens of thousands of text fragments, which described, in graphic detail, child sexual abuse, bestiality, murder, suicide, torture, self-harm, and incest. One might say, "Let the past be the past," but I argue that knowing the development practices of these companies helps us understand more about the nature of the technology and gives us a glimpse into how the company may operate in the future. Put another way: it is telling that OpenAI will not share information about the data in their LLM and perhaps we can chalk that up to proprietary secrecy. It is not, however, in the spirit of their non-profit origin story, however, as their motto claimed, "OpenAI's mission: to build artificial general intelligence (AGI) that is safe and benefits all of humanity" ("About").

Naimh Rowe's November 2023 article for *Wired*, titled "Underage Workers Are Training AI," exposed the ways children from Pakistan, East Africa, Venezuela, India, and the Philippines are signing up for data tagging and data uploading for companies that serve major United States companies, including Amazon, Microsoft Azure, Salesforce, Google, Nvidia, Boeing, and Adobe. Children as young as thirteen bypass the paltry efforts at age verification promised by middleman companies like Toloka, Appen, Clickworker, Teemwork.AI, and OneForma, or their parents legitimately sign up for remote work accounts, and the children take on some of the work in their stead. Rowe reports that "work" in this case includes tagging profanities in texts, determining whether images of naked bodies are lewd or artistic, and uploading their own content (including images of children) for pay that equals approximately one US dollar per day. For many of these children, that money is invaluable, but the work is traumatic and precarious, as accounts are often randomly banned. This exploitation is a necessary component of the generative AI process, and should be at the fore of our minds as we discuss seemingly mundane ideas like writing and reading. Harm is embedded in the development.

The Necessity of Trust

Bender et al. (2021) address another equally important aspect that relates to the readability (and interpretability) of generative AI: "[…] the tendency of human interlocutors to impute meaning where there is none can mislead both [natural language processing] NLP researchers and the general public into taking synthetic text as meaningful" (611). They argue, "[…]even when we don't know the person who generated the language we are interpreting, we build a partial model of who they are and what common ground we think they share with us, and use this in interpreting their words" (616). I think this makes intuitive sense to anyone who is thinking about language and, especially, for people who enjoy playing with language for pleasure or work. What draws people to reading poetry, if not for the pleasure of interpreting rich language where meanings may layer one on top of the other? I would not spend time with a poem such as "Manifesto, or Ars Poetica #2," by Krista Franklin, if I did not trust that the poet had the intention to communicate with the reader. Why do people become so passionate about novels that fail to tie up loose ends, if not because we feel that taking up a work of fiction is the establishment of an essential two-way trust street? Why would readers delight in watching Sherlock Holmes crack the substitution cipher in "The Adventure of the Dancing Men," or spend hundreds of years trying to decipher the impenetrable Voynich manuscript? It must bear noting here that the Enigma machine, the cipher device that enabled Nazi progress in World War II, was broken by the collective efforts of Polish cipher-breakers (including Henryk Zygalski, Jerzy Różycki, and Marian Rejewski) and Bletchley Park, the home base of British cipher breakers, including Alan Turing, the ostensible father of theoretical computer science and progenitor of machine learning.

Naiditch (2010) argues that, in order for people to develop literacy skills, they must not only be taught to comprehend the text, but also to "activate their previous knowledge, make comparisons and connections (analysis), and create new knowledge (synthesis)" (95). If any part of this strategy is interrupted—for example, if the reader cannot trust that they are able to fully comprehend the text, due to any number of reasons including a lack of trust that the text has an interpretable meaning, the reader will not make literacy gains. Before we can inspire students to engage critically with texts, I think we must understand what could be lost in a world where LLM text composition swirls, virtually indistinguishable from human-generated text. Now, I can feel a delightful pushback to this sentiment: "[insert disparaged author's name, or even my name] has never made sense, but people still keep reading their work!" Get your digs in here.

Here in lies one of the many problems, as Bender et al. (2021) note, "[...] if one side of the communication does not have meaning, then the comprehension of the implicit meaning is an illusion arising from our singular human understanding of language (independent of the model)" (616). We know that it has no real meaning, because "an LM is a system for haphazardly stitching together sequences of linguistic forms it has observed in its vast training data, according to probabilistic information about how they combine, but without any reference to meaning: a stochastic parrot" (Bender et al. 2021, 617). Some have argued that this is a bit slanderous on behalf of parrots, who are quite intelligent creatures, but the imagery is sharp and to the point. Where does this leave us, then, if we are looking at the prospect of a world that will be brimming with slop—that is, low-quality regurgitations of text and images produced by generative AI running unchecked?

We are not starting at a very good place, that is certain. I enjoy Fairie's wonderful lists of newspaper clippings that show how Western society, at least, has been complaining about the same things since we had the ability to put our grievances in writing. I use Nicholas Carr's 2008 article, "Is Google Making Us Stupid? What the Internet is Doing to Our Brains," students are apt to talk about the changes in their ability to focus for long periods of times and such. Perhaps it is unfair to burden a single organization (even as powerful and ubiquitous one as Google) with these concerns—perhaps we should consider what it means to now believe that we can … and more importantly, must … have answers at our fingertips. Contemporary responses to Carr's article are fascinating to dive into, especially, "Get Smarter," Jamais Cascio's rebuttal in the same publication one year later. He writes, "Google isn't the problem; it's the beginning of a solution" (Cascio 2009), which seems ill-advised today, given that recent reporting demonstrates that Google Search is overrun with junk content and slop created by generative AI (Vincent 2023). A study conducted by Bevendorff et al. (2024) found "strong correlations between search engine rankings and affiliate marketing, as well as a trend toward simplified, repetitive, and potentially AI-generated content."

More concerning to me is what Cascio (2009) writes next: "In any case, there's no going back. The information sea isn't going to dry up, and relying on cognitive habits evolved and perfected in an era of limited information flow—and limited information access—is futile." Cascio is not the first person to write such a thing, and he certainly isn't the last to do so. In Chapter 4, I will explore the bullying side of generative AI discourse more fully, but I want to touch on this idea of "going back" as it relates to reading. What does it mean to go back to "cognitive habits evolved […] in an era of limited information flow" and is it futile? Or does it not comport with factors that are well outside the scope of generative AI and reading in general? It seems to me that we are in the midst of a mass disability event—more specifically, a mass illiteracy event. According to the 2023 Program for the International Assessment of Adult Competencies (PIAAC) survey results, the percentage of U.S. adults performing at the lowest literacy proficiency increased from 19 percent in 2017 to 28 percent in 2023 ("Highlights of the 2023 U.S. PIAAC Results" 2024). Also, in 2023, the percentage of U.S. adults performing at the lowest level in adaptive problem solving was 32 percent ("Highlights of the 2023

U.S. PIAAC Results" 2024). According to the National Assessment of Educational Progress (NAEP)'s 2024 assessment of literacy in fourth and eighth grades, average scores declined in reading at both grades, and the average reading score for fourth graders in the United States was two points lower than the 2022 average, and five points lower than the 2019 average ("NAEP Reading: Reading Results" 2024).

"The information sea isn't going to dry up" either, because a few very wealthy people have realized that it is in their best interest to keep people distracted trying to either sift through the morass or deluded that they have touched the fingertip of God. But let us take up the idea of "information sea," which suggests to me that "information" is an uncontested good, useful thing, just as "progress" suggests positive forward motion. One need only review "Stochastic Parrots" to understand that data, or "the information sea," is at best useless and at worst, mortally harmful, without powerful human interventions to cull the wheat from the chaff. "An information sea" puts us, today, with spam and slop everywhere; it makes it all the more difficult to find helpful and accurate information because of the firehose of falsehoods or deliberate misinformation being churned into the water. Educators complain that students do not know how to find and vet information because they can remember a time when Google Search brought you top results that made sense, not floods of ads and sponsored posts. People have to do so much more work now, on their own, to vet the information that is shoved at them; there is an even greater need now for people to develop advanced critical thinking skills to swim in this dubiously lauded "information sea." It doesn't need to dry up—we would all be better, though, if we could rid the information sea of garbage patches and pollution. Frankly, when generative AI hype merchants tell me their products can save me time ... *this* sort of industrial tidying actually *would* save me time!

"There's no going back" is also a funny sentiment because there won't be anything to "go back" to, soon, if the uncritical embrace of generative AI continues unabated. And, by the way, we have "gone back," in some instances. We have reversed course. Take, right now, the way phonics is being ushered back into schools, after mounting frustrations with an exclusively whole language learning approach. There remains a debate regarding the efficacy of whole language learning, which should be expected, given that Kantrowitz and Hammill were writing about the "reading wars" for *Newsweek* in 1990. In 1997, Regie Routman wrote this evergreen sentiment: "Across the United States, politicians, policymakers, and the media are having a field day bashing public school" (p. 70). According to researcher Stacey Campbell, "Phonological awareness is particularly beneficial for preschool-aged children [...]. When combined with alphabet knowledge (understanding names, features, details of letters and sounds), phonological awareness training can lead to literacy skills growth" (786). On the other hand, researcher Jennifer V. Stowe (2022) argues for keeping whole language approaches as part of the process, noting the pedagogy's connection to Paulo Freire's philosophies, writing "Whole language and critical pedagogies help us imagine how we can engage with students by using language in ways that are relevant, purposeful, meaningful, and respectful of our students" (18). Unless something profound changes in the environment in which children are learning, it is likely that we will continue to debate these processes and presumably discard phonics once again.

It must also be said that many people do not want to "go back" to everything about a previous era. I do not yearn for the late 70s–early 80s when I was being taught phonics. We were doing plenty of other things terribly. We weren't reading diverse authors, we were stuck in punitive behavior practices, accommodations for children with disabilities were barely discussed ... the list could go on for the length of this book, I am certain. Most people also understand both reading and writing as recursive activities, where the practitioner is best served by returning to the work at different places, forwards and backwards, to reevaluate, reconstitute, and reimagine. We hold this practice up as healthy, leading to better outcomes, be it a greater understanding of a text or a more fully fleshed out written document. Why would we not treat our pedagogy in a similar fashion? I understand that this may be a point of divergence, where I am pitting the philosophy of educators against the philosophy of techno-capitalists—conceivably, if they are coming into my sphere to tell me how to do my job, I will make some recommendations of my own, right back at them. I am delighted to hear that educators are reclaiming phonics as a best practice. I do not feel the need to treat the term "progress" as linear—it should always be recursive. No, I don't want to go back; rather, I want to reclaim the sort of brain activities that put fascism on its heel.

The Necessity of Literacy

To do that, we should go back to the most powerful argument for literacy that I have ever encountered, *Narrative of the Life of Frederick Douglass, an American Slave*. Douglass was born in Maryland in February 1818, into enslavement on a plantation. He escaped his enslavement and became the leading figure in African American civil rights in the nineteenth century, largely through his remarkable gift for persuasive writing and oration. Douglass spends a great deal of time in his *Narrative* explaining the importance and power of literacy; he describes how his enslaver's wife, Mrs. Auld, began to teach him to read when he was a young boy. Upon learning this, Mr. Auld forbids his wife from this activity, "telling her, among other things, that it was unlawful, as well as unsafe, to teach a slave to read" (Douglass 2002, 364). "Unlawful" and "unsafe" are two interesting words, as they relate to the literacy of a child. Douglass, as a perceptive genius, also finds them interesting. "'Unsafe' for whom?" is a fair question. Douglass (2002) expands upon this thought: "It [literacy] would forever unfit him to be a slave. He would at once become unmanageable, and of no value to his master. As to himself, it could do him no good, but a great deal of harm. It would make him discontented and unhappy" (364). When Douglass (2002) hears his enslaver's argument forbidding his literacy, he suddenly understands that what he is hearing is fear, and it ignites him: "What he most dreaded, that I most desired" (365). Douglass understands that his enslaver is afraid that if Douglass can read, he can learn, he can express himself and think critically, and he will be armed to fight back against his enslavement. That is, the bonds of enslavement hold more firmly when a person does not have access to literacy. Literacy is liberating.

Mrs. Auld stops teaching Douglass to read, after her husband's screed, and in fact becomes paranoid and militant if she even suspects that Douglas is in a room alone, possibly with a piece of writing. Douglass is so passionate and intrepid that he entices the poor white children in the area to teach him letters and words; he cobbles together his own literacy education and becomes fully literate despite (and because of) his enslavers' fears. He believes fully that doors will be opened to him if he can read and write, and he was absolutely correct. Douglass (2002) finds his voice as he reads about the liberation of other groups of people; he describes reading tracts on Catholic emancipation thusly, "They gave tongue to interesting thoughts of my own soul, which had frequently flashed through my mind, and died away for want of utterance" (369). Upon his escape from enslavement, Douglass (2002) becomes a subscriber to the *Liberator*, an abolitionist publication, of which he writes, "The paper became my meat and my drink. My soul was set all on fire" (429). Douglass becomes a gifted and prolific author himself, inspiring the abolitionist movement as an emancipated man.

Through Douglass, we can appreciate the raw power of literacy as a whole, that language gives access to critical thinking and, therefore, the pursuit of freedom and self-actualization. Scholar Maryanne Wolfe articulates how important the craft of obtaining and practicing literacy is. That is, it is not only important *that* you obtain and practice literacy—*how* you practice the craft of reading and critical thinking is also important to assess. She describes the thrill of the science of reading: "After all the years of research I have pursued to understand what we do when we retrieve a single word, I still remain in awe of what happens when we read a line of words that elicits our deepest thoughts" (Wolfe 2019, 34). In her book, *Reader, Come Home*, Wolfe takes on the dilemma of reading in the digital age. Though she is writing about the challenges we face with digital media writ large, without a specific emphasis on AI (let alone generative AI), she raises concerns that apply directly to the challenge we face today in this brave new sloppy world. This sentiment is a theme of this book—the issues that feel so raw, so new, are in no way new. We have been talking about declining reading habits for ages. We have been talking about dwindling attention spans and engagement for ages. We have had scholars like Wolfe writing persuasively about what we can and should do, and many educators have tried to implement strategies to improve these declining areas. The speed and the scope of the current changing literacy landscape seem to indicate to me that we are facing an existential crisis—not just in terms of the profession, but in terms of human health and safety. I am moved by the research of Kidd and Birhane (2023) when they write, "People form stronger, longer-lasting beliefs when they receive information from agents that they judge to be confident and knowledgeable, starting in early childhood" (1222). We are so vulnerable, as children, beginning to take in information. One thinks back to Douglass, as a child, learning lessons about literacy from a person he knew was evil, and having the sheer brilliance to *interpret* the messages clearly. We are not all born with such wisdom and acumen, sadly. Most of us are more vulnerable than we realize. Wolfe (2019) notes, "It takes years for deep-reading processes to be formed, and as a society we need to be sure that we are vigilant about their development in our young from a very early age" (38). That vigilance should be invigorating for us older humanities folks, whom Wolfe calls, "the expert readers of our society" (38).

I want to pause here and interrogate the idea of "expert readers," as I believe it is a critical and under-discussed aspect of the generative AI discussion. It bears repeating, again and again: many people who are leading these discussions about how to use generative AI have lived most of their lives before the infiltration of generative AI into the daily digital landscape. Many of those people, myself included, were fortunate to live part-to-most of their lives before the rise of social media and digital inescapability. I learned to read and research while most of my objects of inquiry were paper bound. The models I had to learn to be a scholar were people who embodied the patience and slowness necessary to do critical work. Speed was not foregrounded for me as an English major; indeed, I was afforded the opportunity "to choose to expend the extra millisecond needed to maintain deep reading over time," as Wolfe (2019) describes it (38). When people (who seem to be operating in good faith, and who still privilege human potential at least somewhat) talk about using generative AI, it seems to me like they imagine that all human users will also learn to be "expert readers" either before they interact with generative AI, or that they will develop these skills concurrently with lessons on using generative AI. Generative AI would not take the place of reading; *of course*, people would learn to read, because how else would they know if the generative AI had accurately represented the ideas and arguments of a human writer? Wolfe (2019) reiterates this need: "We must be able to use our own knowledge base to grasp new information and interpret it with inference and critical analysis" (55). She argues that the alternative is bleak, leading us to become susceptible to misinformation and misrepresentations, and, worst of all, we will stop caring whether we are reading truth or lies. We will become utterly numb. Will that numbness come from a true apathy, or from the atrophy our brains will suffer from disuse? She declares, however, "An answer to such scenarios is before our eyes: in the reciprocal relationship between background knowledge and deep reading" (Wolfe 2019, 56).

Certainly, Wolfe (2019) argues that reading is an action-oriented, exercise-based activity that has to be taken on as if part of a health regimen: "Only if we continuously work to develop and use our complex analogical and inferential skills will the neural networks underlying them sustain our capacity to be thoughtful, critical analysts of knowledge, rather than passive consumers of information" (62). Use it or lose it, as it were. She writes, "[…] [T]here is a final moment in the reading act when an arms-wide expanse in the reader's mind open up and all our cognitive and affective processes become the stuff of pure attention and reflection" (67). Those of us who teach in the classroom (or virtually) dream of this kind of comprehensive engagement from our students, ourselves, and our colleagues. To be fully open and simultaneously reflective in an act that is the antithesis of passive and accommodating is to also be full of energy and activity.

Wolfe (2019) goes on: "Cognitively and physiologically, this pause is not a quiet or static time. It is an intensely active moment that can lead us even deeper into insights from the text and beyond […]" (67). Based on Wolfe's lush descriptions, deep reading is an activity that must be taught—it cannot be considered a naturally occurring action. We must begin providing this instruction early and reinforce it throughout the compulsory education process. In truth, we must then find ways to encourage people to continue the practice of deep reading after they leave academia, at whatever student level they depart from us. These ideas are important *regardless* of the rise of generative AI. We are ill-prepared for this moment because we have not cracked the code of inspiring a wide populace to value critical thinking and literacy. As Naiditch (2010) argues, "[…] the development of critical thinking skills is associated to […] making it meaningful to one's context and larger community by relating to it on a personal […] and collective (the classroom, the school, the community or the larger society) level" (98). That responsibility should not fall on the shoulders of the humanities, but I believe these disciplines are the most capable of mounting a public-facing argument for why the labor of thinking is valuable. We need support for those efforts, of course, and I will delve more into that topic in Chapter 4 when I discuss critical alliances we should be exploring.

Ultimately, the debates around generative AI devolve into guesses and admissions of the unknown. The truth is that we are unable to fully "read" AI because of the necrotic secrecy surrounding it. When Holmes says that he cannot make bricks without clay, I am reminded that we cannot make concrete declarations about exactly what generative AI can do to improve our lives, for example, because we are reduced to guessing (an activity against which he strenuously caution)s. Why are we being compelled to pretend these things like transparency are not important?

And why must we spend so much time thinking about generative AI use cases in the first place? "Generative AI is still a solution in search of a problem," the headline of Scott Rosenberg's blog, nails it. On the one hand, it feels very easy right now to be distracted by unnecessary things driven by an unabated greed for more money and more power—I return, repeatedly, to the feeling that generative AI is a distraction, first and foremost, from some very serious things happening in the world. Generative AI seems to also be a useful idiot avatar for advancing populism that is attractive to fascists; namely in the way we are talking about generative AI development in nationalistic terms. Thanks to Sam Altman and crew, we are engaging in a twenty-first century version of the Cold War era "Space Race" between the USSR and the United States. This time, instead of killing dogs, monkeys, and people in an effort to prove intellectual supremacy on an international stage, we have a race to the least-effective software built on pirated data to fill energy-guzzling LLMs that have yet to be accused of efficacy. The product does not matter though, as I will discuss in greater detail as I engage with Zitron's (2023) term, "The Rot Economy"—what matters here is the increase in numbers, be it data centers, data theft, or billions borrowed by angel investors for an undefined project. What if generative AI's highest and greatest purpose is to be an avatar for nationalistic pride that necessitates funneling money into the hands of the one percent with the encouragement of a populace that is content to believe the "abracadabra" of it all?

On the other hand, generative AI represents both the fruits of a culture disinterested with reading and a tool to disadvantage anyone trying to pursue critical reading and thinking. Reading requires trust, at a basic level, that the symbols we encounter have an internal logic and meaning. Why would I struggle to sound out words, understand the definitions, and try to derive coherence from a string of squiggles if not for a bone-deep trust that someone is trying to tell me something?

The Holmesian idea of making bricks without clay is also important to understanding generative AI right now. We cannot make good decisions because we have such little information from the developers. We are left to guess and speculate and fight amongst ourselves. We cannot accurately read the machines because we have scant data that we can trust. It is not that Holmes has no data in the mystery of the Copper Beeches case—parsing out his metaphor, he has the materials to make bricks, such as silt and sand, but he is missing a key ingredient, clay. As Violet Hunter regales Holmes and Watson with information, Holmes gets some data that he needs to form a feeling. He expresses his concern that the available information does not put him at ease, but he cannot give Violet a concrete answer (no pun intended) because he does not have all of the facts, as he is only hearing her side of the story with no opportunity to investigate. Holmes' sense is that things are bad, but without information, he cannot know what course to take or how to specifically advise her. Holmes is not bereft of information; he is bereft of the specific information that would enable him to read the situation fully and clearly. Holmes' hesitation reflects his distrust with the completeness of his reading, and thus, his hesitation to speculate. Without an on-the-ground investigation, Holmes knows nothing about the Copper Beeches, the ruinous child, the ghastly Rucastles, or any other relevant data point in the network of points that comprise and inform the situation.

The obscured network of information that Holmes' faces—and generative AI itself—can best be illuminated through assemblage theory, and, in particular, Jane Bennett (2010)'s theory of vibrant matter. Generative AI is an assemblage comprised of many assemblages; as an assemblage, it is in constant motion, and it resists boundaries; it is comprised of human and non-human components; and it is chaotic. Put plainly, generative AI comes together through the interactions of human and nonhuman (for example, copper) elements, over political and geographic landscapes, and those interactions and elements deserve careful consideration as one is trying to arrive at an understanding of the situation. Bennett's (2010) work on what she calls "vibrant matter" is a critical synthesis of these various strands. The importance lies in Bennett's demonstration of how to "read" assemblages as active events with meaningful relationships between contributors. Bennett explains that she chooses "assemblage," as Deleuze and Guattari use the term, to represent "the kind of relation obtaining between the parts of a volatile but somehow functioning whole" (23), thus accounting for chaos and the ebbs and flows of power when analyzing an event like the North American blackouts in 2003 as "vibrant matter" (21–36).

I concede that it is tempting to find the detective work of parsing through layer after obscured layer in this massive assemblage, or hyperobject, in Timothy Morton's (2013) terminology, frustrating; as Higgs and Stornaiuolo (2024) argue, "The present lack of transparency regarding the role of platforms and algorithms in digital writing is likely to intensify as AI technologies become deeply embedded in composing tools and these features become even less visible to users during the composing experience" (635). Burris and Leander (2024) also take up Bennett's theory, and gesture to this amorphous nature of AI, arguing that it is "[…] difficult to 'see' for how distributed it is across heterogeneous components in space and time, including flows of data, human users, and machine processes that operate at different spatiotemporal scales" (563). I want to push back slightly on the idea of generative AI as a hyperobject—shall we say a *mid*-hyperobject?—because I think the congruencies across model development and bot development mean that we can assemble an encyclopedic knowledge of the how and what. Categorizing the "where" will be the more difficult to see (who is making models, where are the data centers springing up, what communities are being impacted, etc.). That specificity seems far less achievable when considering the hyperobject of climate change, for example. And in the case of generative AI, I think it is certainly difficult to see, yes, but as I have argued previously, the hunt for clarity is not only critical but also explanatory in and of itself.

Burriss and Leander (2024) wisely note that an assemblage/vibrant matter framework allows people to envision AI as part of our lived assemblages rather than an "inert tool," noting, "AI also uses and moves us, relying on the data we generate to operate and shaping—often invisibly—our (literacy) activities" (563–564). Naiditch (2010) encourages us to see agency as fundamental to the literacy acquisition process: "If the reader does not believe that he has an active role in the process, then reading classes are bound to become boring and meaningless, as some students describe them" (99). I want to pause for a moment and consider the human agency in this moment, which does mark generative AI as, again, a bit different from my understanding of a hyperobject. We are encountering more generative AI than we might think, when we use Google Search, shop on Amazon, or engage with a customer service chatbot. I absolutely agree that those interactions take a toll on people, but I think it is different than deliberate engagement with a generative AI tool. Making these different types of relationships visible is a critical first step, and Burriss and Leander (2024) argue that assemblage theory opens the door for critical literacy questions grounded in distributed agency among humans and nonhumans, such as "[…] questions about power and authorship: Who/what writes a text, or is responsible for a text, when AI is involved (e.g., in suggesting or creating text)?" (565). These are excellent questions, and I think the place where I want to continue to push against is treating generative AI with the same wholeness as the human being. Perceiving human creators as part of an assemblage is good and right, but I feel like the image here is too close to the sentient robot fallacy that often attends popular representation of generative AI. In other words, generative AI is not an approximation of a discrete unit in the way a human comes closer to manifesting. While I agree with Burriss and Leander (2024) that perceiving humans as part of a meaning-making assemblage with generative AI gives us an opportunity to "think about 'writers' as confederations rather than individuals, word/image/ sound choice as a joint accomplishment, and the impact of texts as traceable to human–non-human assemblages rather than singular human authors" (565), I resist treating generative AI as a singular entity with discrete agency of its own. I would aspire to break down the assemblages within the assemblage of generative AI, in order to begin to point out a myriad of moments where agency and meaning-making matter are crashing into one another in ways that are less deterministic than simply matter being in frictional movement with other matter.

When it comes to discussions of agency, particularly in the literacy space, Burriss and Leander (2024) make a strong case for interrogating the role of algorithms in what people choose to read, when, and in what context. I believe people are generally aware of algorithms, so much so that the word "algorithm" has a strong negative connotation as a mode of manipulation among many, even when people are unsure of exactly what an algorithm is or where it is at work. Most people have a story to tell about having an audible conversation about a particular pair of shoes, for example, and suddenly being presented with advertisements for that very shoe when they open their smartphone. People seem to often associate algorithms with marketing and capitalism, but algorithms play a crucial role in what we read and the context in which we read it. A prime example of this algorithmic maneuvering is Facebook; thanks to the bravery of whistleblower Frances Haugen, formerly the lead product manager for Civic Misinformation and then with the Counter-Espionage initiative on Facebook, we now know that Facebook determined that inciting anger kept people on the website for longer periods with higher engagement. In an interview with CBS anchor Scott Pelley (2021), Haugen said, "Facebook has realized that if they change the algorithm to be safer, people will spend less time on the site, they'll click on less ads, they'll make less money." During Haugen's testimony before the United States Congress in October 2021 that, "[…] Facebook repeatedly encountered conflicts between its own profits and our safety […and…] consistently resolved those conflicts in favor of its own profits. The result has been a system that amplifies division, extremism, and polarization — and undermining societies around the world" ("Statement" 2021, 2). If this deliberate poisoning of the reading space is not concerning enough, imagine the future we are careening toward with more generative AI embedded in more media. Burriss and Leander (2024) rightly assert that "[w]her our readerly and authorial autonomy begin and end in an AI ecosystem may need to be separated by 'cuts' that allow us to understand our choices as motivated not only by our conscious desires, but also by sometimes hidden algorithmic factors" (566).

Conclusion

As educators concerned with literacy, we teach students how to read everything, including generative AI. Achieving generative AI literacy is challenging, as companies and developers obscure their work, so educators must don their detective hats to suss out truth from fiction. In doing so, they can model for their students critical reading and researching skills, and they can share a deeper understanding of generative AI with their students. Educators can start with the overview of environmental costs and human rights abuses in this chapter and consider the case for literacy as they guide students towards a generative AI literacy that empowers them to make educated choices about the tools and texts around them.

References

"2024 Environmental Sustainability Report." 2024. *Microsoft*. https://www.microsoft.com/en-us/corporate-responsibility/sustainability/report

"A New Approach for Scope 3 Emissions." 2021. *Microsoft*. https://download.microsoft.com/download/7/2/8/72830831-5d64-4f5c-9f51-e6e38ab1dd55/Microsoft_Scope_3_Emissions.pdf

"About." 2024. *OpenAI*. December 20. https://openai.com/about/.

"AI Watch: Global Regulatory Tracker | White & Case LLP." n.d. Accessed February 15, 2025. https://www.whitecase.com/insight-our-thinking/ai-watch-global-regulatory-tracker.

Balashova, Ana. 2024. "Generative AI & Environment: Green Dream or Eco Nightmare?" *Kill the DJ*. February 4. https://killthedj.com/generative-ai-environment-impact/.

Bangalore, Srini, Arjita Bhan, Andrea Del Miglio, Pankaj Sachdeva, Vijay Sarma, Raman Sharma, and Bhargs Srivathsan. 2023. "Why Invest in the Data Center Economy." *McKinsey & Company*. January 17. https://www.mckinsey.com/industries/technology-media-and-telecommunications/our-insights/investing-in-the-rising-data-center-economy.

Bender, Emily M., Timnit Gebru, Angelina McMillan-Major, and Shmargaret Shmitchell. 2021. "On the Dangers of Stochastic Parrots: Can Language Models Be Too Big?" In *Proceedings of the 2021 ACM Conference on Fairness, Accountability, and Transparency*, 610–23. FAccT '21. New York, NY: Association for Computing Machinery. https://doi.org/10.1145/3442188.3445922.

Bennett, Jane. 2010. *Vibrant Matter: A Political Ecology of Things*. Duke University Press.

"Best Practice AI: Developing an Explainability Statement for an AI-Enabled Medical Symptom Checker." n.d. *GOV.UK*. Accessed February 15, 2025. https://www.gov.uk/ai-assurance-techniques/best-practice-ai-developing-an-explainability-statement-for-an-ai-enabled-medical-symptom-checker.

Bevendorff, Janek, Matti Wiegmann, Martin Potthast, and Benno Stein. 2024. "Is Google Getting Worse? A Longitudinal Investigation of SEO Spam in Search Engines." In *Advances in Information Retrieval*, edited by Nazli Goharian, Nicola Tonellotto, Yulan He, Aldo Lipani, Graham McDonald, Craig Macdonald, and Iadh Ounis, 14610:56–71. Lecture Notes in Computer Science. Cham: Springer Nature Switzerland. https://doi.org/10.1007/978-3-031-56063-7_4.

"Blueprint for an AI Bill of Rights | OSTP." October 2022. The White House. Accessed March 24, 2025. https://bidenwhitehouse.archives.gov/ostp/ai-bill-of-rights/.

Bryan, Kenza. 2025. "Microsoft Secures Deal to Restore Amazon Rainforest and Offset AI Emissions." *Financial Times*, January 22, sec. Technology sector. https://www.ft.com/content/3ac7e92f-bea5-4460-8791-23a2697d8b80.

Burriss, Sarah K., and Kevin Leander. 2024. "Critical Posthumanist Literacy: Building Theory for Reading, Writing, and Living Ethically with Everyday Artificial Intelligence." *Reading Research Quarterly* 59 (4): 560–69. https://doi.org/10.1002/rrq.565.

Campbell, Stacey. 2020. "Teaching Phonics without Teaching Phonics: Early Childhood Teachers' Reported Beliefs and Practices." *Journal of Early Childhood Literacy* 20 (4): 783–814. https://doi.org/10.1177/1468798418791001.

Carr, Nicholas. 2008. Is Google Making Us Stupid? What the Internet is Doing to Our Brains. *The Atlantic*, July/August. https://www.theatlantic.com/magazine/archive/2008/07/is-google-making-us-stupid/306868/

Cascio, Jamais. 2009. "Get Smarter." *The Atlantic*, July/August. Accessed February 17, 2025. https://www.theatlantic.com/magazine/archive/2009/07/get-smarter/307548/.

Clark, Brett, and John Bellamy Foster. 2001. "William Stanley Jevons and The Coal Question: An Introduction to Jevons's 'Of the Economy of Fuel.'" *Organization & Environment* 14 (1): 93–98. https://doi.org/10.1177/1086026601141005.

Costa, Pedro. 2018. "Conversing with Personal Digital Assistants: On Gender and Artificial Intelligence." *Journal of Science and Technology of the Arts*, September, 59–72 Páginas. https://doi.org/10.7559/CITARJ.V10I3.563.

David, Emilia. 2023. "George R.R. Martin and Other Authors Sue OpenAI for Copyright Infringement." *The Verge*. September 20. https://www.theverge.com/2023/9/20/23882140/george-r-r-martin-lawsuit-openai-copyright-infringement.

David, Emilia. 2024. "Sarah Silverman's Lawsuit against OpenAI Partially Dismissed." *The Verge*. February 13. https://www.theverge.com/2024/2/13/24072131/sarah-silverman-paul-tremblay-openai-chatgpt-copyright-lawsuit.

Dean, Grace. 2023. "A Lawsuit Claims OpenAI Stole 'massive Amounts of Personal Data,' Including Medical Records and Information about Children, to Train ChatGPT." Business Insider. Accessed March 21, 2025. https://www.businessinsider.com/openai-chatgpt-generative-ai-stole-personal-data-lawsuit-children-medical-2023-6.

Donelan, Michelle. 2024. "A Pro-Innovation Approach to AI Regulation—Government Response to Consultation." *Department for Science, Innovation and Technology*.

Douglass, Frederick. 2002. "Narrative of the Life of Frederick Douglass." In *The Classic Slave Narratives*, edited by Henry Louis Gates, Jr., 323–436. Signet Classic.

Doyle, Arthur Conan. 1892. "Adventures of Sherlock Holmes. XII.—The Adventures of the Copper Beeches." *Strand Magazine: An Illustrated Monthly* 3 (01): 613–628. http://proxy.lib.odu.edu/login?url=https://www.proquest.com/historical-periodicals/adventures-sherlock-holmes/docview/3977486/se-2.

Eisikovits, Nir. 2023. "AI Is an Existential Threat—Just Not the Way You Think." *The Conversation*. July 5. https://theconversation.com/ai-is-an-existential-threat-just-not-the-way-you-think-207680.

Elder, Alexis. 2022. "Siri, Stereotypes, and the Mechanics of Sexism." *Feminist Philosophy Quarterly* 8 (3/4). https://doi.org/10.5206/fpq/2022.3/4.14294.

Fairie, Paul. [@paulisci.bsky.social]. 2025. A Brief History of Kids Today Are Lazy. View: March 31. https://bsky.app/profile/paulisci.bsky.social/post/3llpevyi3f22n. [Post]. Bluesky.
"Generative Artificial Intelligence (AI)." 2025. *Harvard University Information Technology*. https://www.huit.harvard.edu/ai.
"Generative Artificial Intelligence | Center for Teaching Innovation." 2025. *Cornell University Center for Teaching Innovation*. https://teaching.cornell.edu/generative-artificial-intelligence.
Higgs, Jennifer M., and Amy Stornaiuolo. 2024. "Being Human in the Age of Generative AI: Young People's Ethical Concerns about Writing and Living with Machines." *Reading Research Quarterly* 59 (4): 632–50. https://doi.org/10.1002/rrq.552.
"Highlights of the 2023 U.S. PIAAC Results." 2024. NCES. *National Center for Education Statistics*. 2024. https://nces.ed.gov/surveys/piaac/2023/national_results.asp.
"HireVue AI Explainability Statement." 2022. *Hirevue.Com*. March 31. https://www.hirevue.com/press-release/hirevue-launches-ai-explainability-statement-in-hr-industry-first.
IEEE Public Safety Technology. 2025. "Ethical Considerations in the Use of Facial Recognition for Public Safety—IEEE Public Safety Technology Initiative." *IEEE.Org*. https://publicsafety.ieee.org/topics/ethical-considerations-in-the-use-of-facial-recognition-for-public-safety.
Jevons, William Stanley. 1895. *The Coal Question; An Inquiry Concerning the Progress of the Nation, and the Probable Exhaustion of Our Coal Mines*. Macmillan and Co.
Kantrowitz, Barbara, and Roxie Hammill. 1990. "The Reading Wars." *Newsweek*.
Kidd, Celeste, and Abeba Birhane. 2023. "How AI Can Distort Human Beliefs." *Science* 380 (6651): 1222–1223. https://doi.org/10.1126/science.adi0248.
Kraft, Amy. 2016. "Microsoft Shuts down AI Chatbot, Tay, after It Turned into a Nazi." *CBS News*. March 25. https://www.cbsnews.com/news/microsoft-shuts-down-ai-chatbot-after-it-turned-into-racist-nazi/.
"Leading Countries by Number of Data Centers as of March 2024." n.d. *Statista*. Accessed March 2, 2025. https://www.statista.com/statistics/1228433/data-centers-worldwide-by-country/.
Lehane, Christopher. 2025. "OpenAI's OSTP Submission." *OpenAI.com*.
Luccioni, Alexandra Sasha, Emma Strubell, and Kate Crawford. 2025. "From Efficiency Gains to Rebound Effects: The Problem of Jevons' Paradox in AI's Polarized Environmental Debate." *arXiv*. https://doi.org/10.48550/arXiv.2501.16548.
Masley, Andy. 2025. "Using ChatGPT Is Not Bad for the Environment." Substack newsletter. *The Weird Turn Pro* (blog). January 13. https://andymasley.substack.com/p/individual-ai-use-is-not-bad-for.

"Meta Selects Northeast Louisiana as Site of $10 Billion Artificial Intelligence Optimized Data Center; Governor Jeff Landry Calls Investment 'A New Chapter' for State." 2024. *Louisiana Economic Development.* December 4. https://www.opportunitylouisiana.gov/news/meta-selects-northeast-louisiana-as-site-of-10-billion-artificial-intelligence-optimized-data-center-governor-jeff-landry-calls-investment-a-new-chapter-for-state.

Morton, Timothy. 2013. *Hyperobjects: Philosophy and Ecology after the End of the World.* The University of Minnesota Press.

Muller, Wesley. 2025. "Louisiana Pays More for Electricity from One of the Least Reliable Grids, Audit Finds." *Louisiana Illuminator* (blog). January 24. https://lailluminator.com/2025/01/24/louisiana-pays-more-for-electricity-from-one-of-the-least-reliable-grids-audit-finds/.

Maurer, Roy. 2021. "HireVue Discontinues Facial Analysis Screening." SHRM, February 3. https://www.shrm.org/topics-tools/news/talent-acquisition/hirevue-discontinues-facial-analysis-screening.

"NAEP Reading: Reading Results." n.d. Accessed February 17, 2025. https://www.nationsreportcard.gov/reports/reading/2024/g4_8/.

Naiditch, Fernando. 2010. "Critical Pedagogy and the Teaching of Reading for Social Action." *Critical Questions in Education* 1:94–107.

O'Brien, Matt. 2024. "Ireland Embraced Data Centers That the AI Boom Needs. Now They're Consuming Too Much of Its Energy." *The Associated Press.* December 19. https://apnews.com/article/ai-data-centers-ireland-6c0d63cbda3df740cd9bf2829ad62058.

Pelley, Scott. 2021. "Facebook Whistleblower Frances Haugen Details Company's Misleading Efforts on 60 Minutes." *CBS News.* October 4. https://www.cbsnews.com/news/facebook-whistleblower-frances-haugen-misinformation-public-60-minutes-2021-10-03/.

Rosenberg, Scott. 2024. "We Still Don't Know What Generative AI Is Good For." *Axios.* April 24. https://www.axios.com/2024/04/24/generative-ai-why-future-uses.

Roth, Emma. 2024. "Authors Sue Anthropic for Training AI Using Pirated Books." *The Verge.* August 20. https://www.theverge.com/2024/8/20/24224450/anthropic-copyright-lawsuit-pirated-books-ai.

Routman, Regie. 1997. "Back to the Basics of Whole Language." *Educational Leadership* 54 (5): 70.

Rowe, Niamh. 2023. "Underage Workers Are Training AI." *Wired*, November 15. https://www.wired.com/story/artificial-intelligence-data-labeling-children/.

Saenko, Kate. 2023. "Is Generative AI Bad for the Environment? A Computer Scientist Explains." *GovTech.* May 25. https://www.govtech.com/artificial-intelligence/is-generative-ai-bad-for-the-environment-a-computer-scientist-explains.

Scherer, Matt. 2022. "HireVue 'AI Explainability Statement' Mostly Fails to Explain What It Does." *Center for Democracy and Technology* (blog). September 8. https://cdt.org/insights/hirevue-ai-explainability-statement-mostly-fails-to-explain-what-it-does/.

Singer, Peter. 1997. "The Drowning Child and the Expanding Circle | New Internationalist." April 5. https://newint.org/features/1997/04/05/peter-singer-drowning-child-new-internationalist.

Smith, Brad, and Melanie Nakagawa. 2023. "Accelerating Sustainability with AI: A Playbook." *Microsoft On the Issues*. November 16. https://blogs.microsoft.com/on-the-issues/2023/11/16/accelerating-sustainability-ai-playbook/.

Spenser, Thomas, and Siddharth Singh. 2024. "What the Data Centre and AI Boom Could Mean for the Energy Sector—Analysis." *IEA*. October 18. https://www.iea.org/commentaries/what-the-data-centre-and-ai-boom-could-mean-for-the-energy-sector.

"Statement of Frances Haugen." 2021. Washington, D.C.: United States Senate Committee on Commerce, Science and Transportation. https://www.commerce.senate.gov/services/files/FC8A558E-824E-4914-BEDB-3A7B1190BD49.

Stowe, Jennifer V. 2022. "Connecting Whole Language and Critical Pedagogy." *Talking Points* 33 (2): 11–19. https://doi.org/10.58680/tp202231856.

Strubell, Emma, Ananya Ganesh, and Andrew McCallum. 2019. "Energy and Policy Considerations for Deep Learning in NLP." *arXiv*. https://doi.org/10.48550/arXiv.1906.02243.

Sweet, Julie. 2024. "Three Opportunities and Actions to Harness the Power of Generative AI to Enable the Energy Transition." In *Fostering Effective Energy Transition*. World Economic Forum.

Vincent, James. 2023. "AI is Being Used to Generate Whole Spam Sites." *The Verge*, May. https://www.theverge.com/2023/5/2/23707788/ai-spam-content-farm-misinformation-reports-newsguard.

Wolfe, Maryanne. 2019. *Reader, Come Home: The Reading Brain in a Digital World*. Harper.

Woods, Heather Suzanne. 2018. "Asking More of Siri and Alexa: Feminine Persona in Service of Surveillance Capitalism." *Critical Studies in Media Communication* 35 (4): 334–49. https://doi.org/10.1080/15295036.2018.1488082.

Zitron, Ed. 2023. "The Rot Economy." *Ed Zitron's Where's Your Ed At*. February 9. https://www.wheresyoured.at/the-rot-economy/.

Zitron, Ed. 2025. "Monologue: The Super Bowl Showed That Generative AI Is Washed." Better Offline. Accessed February 14. https://podcasts.apple.com/us/podcast/monologue-the-super-bowl-showed-that-generative-ai-is/id1730587238?i=1000692131977.

CHAPTER 4

"And Then there Were None": Generative AI and Labor

Abstract Stepping away from the immediacy of the classroom, this chapter considers the humanities as a profession and the role educators play as laborers within the higher education industrial complex. This chapter interrogates the role time and speed play in our working conditions and the changes that are being proposed to those conditions. This chapter suggests that we think about the way "incapacitating technocapitalism" might be a framework that imperils our most essential work: teaching critical reading and writing skills.

Keywords Labor · Union · Generative AI

Introduction

In almost every interaction I have had with someone who feels optimistic about the way generative AI can transform our world, the essential pitch boils down to how generative AI will save me time. Generative AI saves a great amount of time, I am told, to free me up to do more important things, or things that should be a higher priority for me. According to the Thomson Reuters Institutes' "2024 Future of Professionals Report," "54% were most excited about the benefit of saving time through AI technology, particularly by freeing them from necessary but repetitive tasks."

D. J. Gavin, *Generative AI and the Future of the Humanities*,
https://doi.org/10.1007/978-3-032-06534-6_4

So much money and energy (human and carbon) has been spent on developing generative AI … just to save me, the lowly consumer, time—and specifically time that I should spend on matters of more consequence to me or matters that require a higher level of human thought. It seems as though we have been under siege for generations. I think about Violet Hunter in "The Adventure of the Copper Beeches"—I am so tired of being tired, and I will jump at any chance to experience relief that I am more and more likely to eschew a deep dive into the information available that may dissuade me from availing myself of the tempting "solution."

The Algorithm "knows" me, so ads on LinkedIn and other social media sites have promised me that generative AI can be used in the form of chatbots that can answer students' questions, bots that can tutor them, bots that can draft lesson plans and discussion questions, and even bots that can offer students' feedback on their writing assignments. Assuredly, as IBM puts it, "AI is not yet loading the dishwasher after supper—but can help create a legal brief, a new product design, or a letter to grandma" (*AI Examples & Business Use Cases | IBM* 2024). Grandparents everywhere, you have been warned—treat letters from your grandkids with great suspicion.

The tasks being automated by AI are skill-based; they are just often skills people don't enjoy. At the same time, then, people must still acquire and practice those skills to perform quality control and take on the tasks when the computers fail: thus, a conundrum.

Outsourcing into Oblivion

We outsource so much of ourselves now. We task these things with doing so much of the grunt work of life, but we may not think about the consequences. When we are without our technology—the smartphone, the laptop, the internet especially—our concept of life changes. It is not just inconvenience—it is incapacity. We go from "having the world at our fingertips" (a problematic misconception) to being functionally inert. That is not just from skills attrition, though that is certainly part of the story. We have disposed of the old technologies that once carried us through. For example, if you lose your smartphone, you may not be able to find a pay phone in the United States. You may even have a challenge getting access to a landline. If you need to look up a phone number, you will have difficulty finding a paper phone book. We have changed our material lives on the basis of, one might argue, a false premise that current technology is not only an unalloyed good but will survive indefinitely.

Let us return, then, to the Luddites—people who understood the value of their craft, why their craft was important to the industry, the ways in which technology could support the quality of their craft, and who were ultimately prepared to stand up in defense of good work. If an organization is proposing the elimination of jobs in favor of using generative AI, I think laborers must stand up and fight for that work. In truth, generative AI is not taking on clearly dangerous manual labor; there are no good reasons for generative AI to eliminate jobs wholesale.

The trickier position reveals itself when laborers are told that their workplace will begin integrating generative AI into their processes. People should listen for buzzy phrases like "saving time," or "making your life easier." These sound like good ideas, but they obscure threats to both employment and skill development. It may be very difficult to even get a seat at the table when decisions are being made, but it is not impossible. In all cases, it is critical that laborers research and understand the types of generative AI products that could be considered for implementation and learn as much about them (or that type of technology) as far in advance as possible. At present, many people talk about generative AI and few people take the time to truly understand the scope of generative AI's impact—laborers should make themselves indispensable by coming to their employer with data-driven information.

When laborers are evaluating the presence of generative AI in their workforce, they should consider a few basic questions:

- What exactly is the work being automated?
- What human work went into that task or process?
- If that labor is no longer being done by people, who is tasked with quality control?
- What jobs and, importantly, what experiences are being cut out? How will people continue to learn those "low level" skills to check against the AI's work?

"Incapacitating Technocapitalism"

Luis Suarez-Villa (2012) defines "technocapitalism" as a new kind of capitalism that marries technology and corporate power, and argues that "[i]ts global reach reflects the ethos of a new era in which corporate power, technology and science have become deeply entwined and all-encompassing, moved by a seemingly unstoppable drive for control over everyone and over all of the earth's resources" (1). I want to highlight to the way this technology is not only being forced upon us, demanding customers, but also making us illiterate in the process. That is a key part of this technology's harm pattern. It is fair to say that other technologies have had an impact on our literacies, but due to the speed and scope of the generative AI pervasion, I want to foreground the incapacitating nature of this particular threat. Who benefits from a populace that can no longer read and write effectively?

I raised the bogeyman, NaNoWriMo, in Chap. 2, when I thought fondly back on its humble origins, what it told me about the spirit of creativity that still longs for community, and how the internet facilitated that community being able to "gather" with no earthly challenges like time and space. What a perfect use case! And yet, the story of NaNoWriMo's debasement is also an example of how the commodification of creativity, the demanding sprawl that accompanies technology, and a loss of the original mission can degrade even the most innocuous of intentions. In 1999, a few friends decided to challenge each other to write –by 2006, NaNoWriMo was a 501c3, a nonprofit that could raise money, host hundreds of thousands of writers on their sprawling message boards, and fund resources like their Young Writers Program (Wang 2025). In less than ten years, the entire size and scope of the original idea (committing oneself to writing lots of material in a short time frame to hopefully ignite and nurture one's creativity) became a multi-pronged organization requiring intensive labor with multiple laborers at multiple levels, dealing with an international audience of all ages. Maybe it was inevitable that in 2023, allegations would arise regarding the moderation or lack thereof in a NaNoWriMo online forum called "Christian Teens Together," suggesting that the moderator was not only lax but also the owner of a fetish website allegedly featuring minors, and thus interactions with teens and younger children was not advisable. A timeline of accusations and events is hosted on a public Google Doc at nanoscandal.com, including accusations of abuse on the Young Writers Program forums.

Within a year, the heads of NaNoWriMo attempted to course correct and ban minors from the site at large, but the damage was more than done. Then, NaNoWriMo attempted to take a stand on the generative AI question: in August 2024, the head team released a statement that not only accepted the use of AI but stated that criticism of the use of AI was classist and ableist. Board members resigned, with Daniel José Older pointing out that ProWritingAid, an AI-powered writing tool, had recently become a sponsor of NaNoWriMo (Wang 2025). Now, there are some regional groups continuing with the original mission of inspiring writing, but they are unfederated and disconnected from the larger, money-fueled operation. Those groups are powered by the same laborers, who had donated their time to nurturing their small groups over the years. The work on the ground remained critical and they stayed in service of the mission.

These days, I often think about a verse from Bruce Springsteen's "Youngstown," a song about poverty in Appalachia that also recognizes the industrial exploitation that materially benefited the wealthy. Springsteen sings:

Seven hundred tons of metal a day.
Now sir you tell me the world's changed.
Once I made you rich enough.
Rich enough to forget my name.

Springsteen's nameless iron worker's anger puts me in mind of the hurt I hear coming out of articles like Wang's, where people just wanted to keep working on their writing, not be entangled in a multi-level non-profit juggernaut. Similarly, we are not being asked *if* we want generative AI; we are having it inserted into our media and the extensions of ourselves, as McLuhan would suggest. Our bodies serve as content necessary to continually enrich the heads of these tech companies, and there is either no interest in the literacy fallout ... or there is actually an *investment* in such a fallout.

Now, let us set aside the company's (or higher ed. administration's) motivations for adopting generative AI, temporarily. Understanding motivation is an exceedingly important aspect of the negotiation process, but at first, let the focus be purely on laborer and skill impact. There are surely repetitive processes that do not impart any skill whatsoever, nor are they useful from a quality-check standpoint—from the standpoint of labor, automation in this case would seem innocuous (but for the fact that, at least presently, generative AI is still a highly polluting enterprise, and thus, cannot be fully innocuous).

More likely, the automation, or the removal of certain tasks, will impact the laborer in terms of skills acquisition and development. One example: Zrinka Stahuljak, a professor of Medieval Studies in California, uploaded all her research material to ChatGPT. The bot produced lecture notes, slides, rubrics, and more, including materials for her teaching assistants to use during their breakout sessions with students (Brenner 2024). At first blush, this may seem brilliant—the seasoned educator is able to offload an incredibly laborious task and, presumably, continue her researching and teaching work for other projects. However, this one act did not necessarily save the professor a great deal of time, as (hopefully) she closely reviewed the materials. Most consequently, it took away an opportunity for the teaching assistants, graduate students looking for professional development as future educators themselves. The work of developing support materials, of thinking through those little moments of student interaction, may seem like mind-numbing minutia for faculty who have been in the classroom for years. The seasoned faculty members may feel like they are unburdening the graduate student, giving them the break that the faculty member wishes they were given. The faculty member may be conscious of the way graduate students are stretched thin trying to survive with ever-more-meager funding and is trying to be supportive by taking at least one task off the graduate student's plate. Such kindness is laudable, and yet, it removes a learning opportunity for the graduate student and it fails to address the core issues of why graduate students, among other precarious groups, are facing challenges that educators who developed professionally in the 1980s and 1990s may have not experienced.

Maybe it is silly to worry about teaching assistants and their ability to develop professionally—there are fewer and fewer tenure-track jobs in the humanities. I would still like to worry about them and consider their roles in the academic landscape as integral to the dissemination of information. Institutions have also relied on graduate student labor primarily as an inexpensive way to carry forth the work of teaching lower-level courses, not as much for the opportunity for students to grow their understanding of pedagogy, but as relief for overworked faculty who may need to (or prefer to) teach upper level courses. We must continue the fight against the casualization and exploitation of the profession, which contributes to undermining the high quality of instruction we know we can deliver.

We also must consider the impact of generative AI adoption on the academic publishing industry. Kathryn Palmer (2025), writing for *Inside Higher Ed*, revealed that publishing powerhouses Wiley, Elsevier, and

Springer Nature have "all announced the adoption of generative AI–powered tools or guidelines, including those designed to aid scientists in research, writing and peer review." I completely understand why organizations would favor accelerating the pace at which academics produce, and especially review, work. We have either experienced or heard stories about papers being stuck in peer review hell for months, if not years. The peer review process is labor intensive for the reviewers, to be sure, and uncompensated financially. If generative AI could promise to move papers along quicker, or give academics an opportunity to research and write even quicker, that would be a boon for publishers whose commodity is based on the free labor of academics, who are compelled to feed those companies in a *publish or perish* fake economy. But, of course, at what cost? I would point to every chapter prior to explain my profound concern and anger at this proposition. And yet, who can afford to opt out? Is there even an opt-out possibility?

On that note, we can learn from the Luddites, too—slop poisons the well for everyone. If owners are allowed to hire unskilled workers and let them use generative AI tools to make stabs at humanities-driven work, the valuation of those skills will crater even more than they already have. The humanities have been underfunded and ignored for decades. We have been told that our graduates (a declining population, to be sure) do not experience the same level of career success that peers in other disciplines do, even though they still do earn more than non-degree holders (June 2023). We cannot permit people to continue to insist that anyone can simply wave their hand and create something as important and powerful as one with developed critical skills can. We cannot think so little of our own work that we cede our power to create, innovate, and educate.

Communicating Value

What does it look like to truly value one's work and to share that valuation with society? First, we should do more auditing of our labor and isolate where the skills that the humanities teach play a role. We can self-audit in our own lives, develop rubrics for other people to use to audit themselves, and find creative ways to report the findings. This, of course, is a conundrum, as one of the great obstacles currently is a lack of traditional modes of communication—the three big television networks are a distant memory, we do not listen to the same five radio stations, and print media is long dead.

First, however, we do need to convince ourselves that our skills are eminently relevant to a wider scope of societal need. On the surface, it seems we are united, but that is certainly a mask. Disciplines that authentically believed in the necessity of the skills developed through their practice would not have permitted the casualization and de-professionalization of the profession that has occurred over the past 50 years. A discipline that believed in the necessity of its skill set, such as "English," would not fail to evolve as it became obvious that, while the skills were inherently necessary, the pedagogy needed to reflect the changing face of the student population and the developing modes of communication. We are in a more precarious situation than we should be because the standard-bearers of the humanities have not demanded that the disciplines make it difficult for anyone to fail to take them seriously. During a panel session at the 2025 MLA conference in New Orleans, a panelist said that English professors had mastered the skill of teaching writing and had no need to change in light of the rise of generative AI. I was stunned. If we had all mastered the art of teaching writing, surely the word would have spread like wildfire, and our classes would be overflowing. Because surely, if we've mastered the art of teaching writing, we have also conveyed the importance of strong writing skills, either explicitly or implicitly, and that is why the students are beating down our doors. That is why administrators are rushing to hire more full-time faculty, so senior faculty can mentor them in these areas with robust expertise.

I see the opposite happening, and I see most of my labor efforts directed at stemming the tide of "adjunctification" because there is a pervasive belief that anyone off the street who can speak can probably write and therefore can teach writing. This must be true, because we would not treat writing experts as poorly as we treat adjuncts, giving them little to no resources that would enable them to effectively do the job asked of them. We would not have our most vital writing course taught by people being abused and stretched so thin. And we certainly would not be entertaining the idea that anything other than a human being could guide another human being through the hilarious pitfalls of learning to write, especially in the raggamuffin English language. We have not countered the rising tide of distaste for the humanities—if anything, we have "leaned in" and acceded that, in fact, we are less important to students, to the college, and to society. Surely some of that "leaning in" was in an effort to placate a world that, unfortunately, does not seem to be interested in nurturing the critical thinking skills of people. Maybe we thought we could operate under the radar, and that would take some of the heat off. Whatever the case, our tactics have not worked to our advantage, and most certainly, not the students' or society's advantage. Thus, we in the humanities are meeting this moment off balance, causing more challenges for ourselves because we were not the picture of stability to begin with.

We must get aggressive, now, about telling the story of the work we do to the public. This work will entail a grassroots campaign that will certainly need to exploit social media and family-friend networks on as grand a scale as any federal political campaign. While waiting for a Board of Trustees meeting to start, a local politician asked me what my role at the college was. Upon my answer, he smiled, thanked me, and proceeded to tell me all about the role writing plays in his trucking and construction business. He told me that he was often frustrated with new hires, because writing effective reports was how his company brought in reimbursement revenue, and he treasured the employees who had the skills to deliver the most comprehensive reports that led to more money in the coffers. Surely, we all have stories like this—we must capitalize on them and weaponize them. Thus, the audit. We must make these skills hyper-visible, and we must reflect on how we are presenting our labor, in the form of teaching, as accessible to the widest populations of students as possible.

To this end, we cannot allow the hype merchants to persuade us that, again, the only way to handle the rise of generative AI is to capitulate, to accede and fold. We do not have to carry water for technocapitalists to be taken seriously. In fact, the harder we lean into the tech hype demands, the easier it will be to see our skills and disciplines as midgrade and as disposable. We have made the argument that we are malleable—too malleable in the wrong ways. We should be adaptable, but not to external forces that do not value the skills we know are critical.

We should also think in terms of what skills are critical to the jobs we hope to protect from the intrusion of generative AI, as I referenced earlier in terms of teaching assistants. What skills, say, in the marketing departments of colleges, will be lost through the adoption of generative AI? Do we have throngs of entry-level jobs that are, in part, designed for laborers to either gain or develop their skills, in anticipation of advancement?

One consideration to bear in mind—it may be a challenge for experienced people to think back to the sort of entry level skill acquisitions you experienced in early jobs. Tech hype merchants seem to count on this very brand of amnesia, as I am routinely hearing established professional people say that their skills will certainly not be impacted by their use of generative AI. Let us set aside whether or not that claim is ultimately true—it is certainly the case that people over the age of 30 have had a solid time prior to Fall 2022 to hone those writing and reading skills. Even if they haven't mastered those skills, they have had more than 20 years of opportunities to develop and mature with no or limited interference from generative AI. Younger generations will not have such affordances. They are imperiled now, and they will not be given an opportunity to focus on skill development as generative AI is deployed to "save them" the time they might "waste" on learning such skills.

It might be fair to question here if I am simply advocating that younger generations should suffer because I suffered—certainly, in academia, we have imposed generational misery built on the heuristic that if I had to do it, you have to do it, whether it was beneficial or not. "It's not fair because I had to do it," senior academics will suggest, if we look for ways to mitigate harmful gatekeeping efforts like excessive promotion and tenure measures, or even overly laborious hiring practices. If generative AI offered an opportunity for the alleviation of true "grunt work"—work that did not involve writing thoughtfully or reviewing data and processes, there might be a place for it. What I see instead are exaltations that generative AI can be used to write pesky recommendation letters for students and colleagues and grade papers. One of the first advertisements I remember on LinkedIn was for a bot that would take my rubric and use it as the basis for automated feedback on student papers. While I cannot remember what product was being advertised at the time, I remember having an instantaneous feeling of euphoria at the idea of outsourcing grading. I dislike grading immensely, and it took me a long time to figure out why I found it so unnatural and off-putting. It wasn't until I started tutoring in a writing center to supplement my adjunct work that I realized my disdain for grading wasn't rooted in dislike for the labor, it was a disdain for the process and context. I realized that I really liked talking with someone about what they had written, particularly when a grade wasn't on the line. I liked pointing out how to potentially fix an awkward sentence—I did not like trying to figure out how to take off points for lack of clarity. I enjoyed the dialogue with the novice writer—I got frustrated trying to scribble complex suggestions and questions into the margins of assignments. I enjoyed helping novice writers find things to feel good about in their writing and find ways to strengthen their skills, and taking points off a final grade for infractions was in no way accomplishing my teaching goals.

In a blog titled "Using AI Tools to Give Feedback on High School Students' Writing," which evaluates the BriskTeaching and MagicSchool AI tools, a veteran high school teacher writes, "As a writing teacher I want to give all of my high school students specific detailed feedback about their drafts, but there is just one of me and more than 140 of them" (Roberts 2024). This is the first sentence and feels like it should lead to a much different labor assessment. The problem here cannot be solved by adding generative AI to the mix—this veteran teacher may be opening herself up to having far more than 140 students if she demonstrates that she can make it seem like students are getting the full breadth of her expertise. Of course, we know that the students are not getting the full breadth of her expertise, because it is impossible for her to give 140-plus students detailed feedback on their drafts. That's the fullest expression of her expertise: the detailed feedback that only she can offer. The solution should not dilute her expertise by substituting generative AI; the solution should be to reduce the teacher-student ratio to a manageable load, where she can deliver her expertise in a manner that truly benefits the students. She is not the only expert in this area, so hire more writing experts to teach the remaining students at ratios that make sense. There are reasons why this isn't happening, but overcoming those reasons should be the united focus of laborers rather than adopting technology that only makes it easier for upper administrators to further disenfranchise laborers. Because that is what this is—this expert educator is being kept farther and farther away from using her expertise to immediately benefit students. Students, who we have been told, suffered under the lockdown time of the COVID19 pandemic, and who presumably need more human interaction, not less. Yes, it is easier to adopt the hot new product rather than continuously and potentially fruitlessly rally against an administration hell-bent on saving money through resisting new hires. However, we are suggesting repeatedly that our expertise can be outsourced or at least spread thin through generative AI means to only half-nurture student talent. That seems like a disservice to us, to the profession, and to the students.

Another common usage I perceive is using generative AI for writing letters of recommendation. Let us stop and consider why letters of recommendation are so time-consuming. Too many students, too many other service responsibilities, a sense that these letters do not get read closely anyway ... and now, a pretty good sense that applications are being run through generative AI programs anyways, so why not have generative AI "talk" to generative AI?

I borrow this chapter's title from the classic Agatha Christie novel, and I suppose I am trying to channel a bit of the macabre: many people have joked that tech developers today have watched movies like *Minority Report* and *2001: A Space Odyssey* and said, "These are great ideas!" Surely, there is a pervasive feeling that administrators would love nothing more than to have one educator per 1000 students, where the educator has the illusion that generative AI is enabling her to promulgate her expertise authentically. She will have a job, she reasons, and the humanities will still be "taught." There is a second reason for the invocation to Christie's book, and please do forgive the spoilers: the murderer, Mr. Justice Wargrave, a retired criminal judge, finds himself on the precipice of death and decides that he will act out his fantasy of being both judge and executioner. Criminals that he has deemed unpunished for their crimes are lured to a remote island where he dispatches them one by one, leaving the remaining people to exist in a state of terror, waiting for their end to come. The judge has thus become the criminal, and as he takes out one after the other, I am reminded of the way we can turn on ourselves, and turn on each other, in this chaotic and frenetic time.

We seem to be assuring ourselves that we are moving into a time where the AI will do the writing, and we (and our students) will be doing the editing. That is the most acceptable viewpoint for many people. Because the current generation of educators is already in command of the faculties of reading and writing, this seems plausible. I have made the argument elsewhere that, very soon, generations will not be in possession of these skills. In this framework, I am concerned with how we are obliterating our profession even without the help of higher education administrations.

The more we demonstrate how effective we are at managing generative AI, the more humanities faculty will be managers and not educators. There will be a few sources of curriculum, and people will be tasked with managing the generative AI's delivery of said curriculum. If this seems far-fetched, consider the current academic job market. Consider your own institution if you are affiliated with one in any capacity. How many tenure-track faculty positions are currently filled? How many lines are open and actively being recruited? How many people are classified as staff positions? And how many of those staff positions teach in some capacity? If tenure-track faculty become managers of generative AI, that work can be done by someone who is not classified as a faculty member. The faculty member—an expensive person who, by virtue of tenure and the principles of academic freedom, is in a far more secure position than any other employee group—is made redundant. Generative AI course packs will become the norm, with a select few faculty kept on as discipline experts to make sure everything is kept in line.

You may say this was the same fear expressed when Massive Open Online Courses (MOOCs) debuted in the early 2000s, and I would agree! Here, I think, is the primary difference between the MOOCs and our current situation: money and power. With generative AI, we see people like Sam Altman and Elon Musk at the helm—people who have invested untold amounts of money into LLM projects and who will, come hell or high water, recoup that money and double it. They have a level of power that MOOC developers could not dream of, and generative AI is in no way beholden to the province of education—though I think it is vital to the developers of generative AI that education falls in line and adopts it.

We also see a different kind of tolerance for the distance technology puts between people. Even though people believed at the time that students were being grotesquely harmed by the kind of online learning that was necessitated by the COVID19 pandemic in 2020, we still see students flocking to online courses. Even students who literally live on campuses. While some school districts are putting restrictions and bans on smartphones, many are still operating under the "a Chromebook for every child, and a child for every Chromebook" mentality. The presence of screens is not an anathema, and while MOOCs were impersonal, generative AI does not have to be. Thus, the push to have educators adopt generative AI into their pedagogy willingly—we can curate a feeling of trust, acceptance, and even dependence on generative AI at a young age if we attach generative AI to the personal touch of an in-person educator.

I am often reminded of the logo for a chain of restaurants, Red Hot & Blue. When I lived in Dallas, I found it so lovely to take a break from Texas-style barbecue and enjoy their Memphis-style wares. I couldn't, however, walk in without commenting, grimly, about the signage for the restaurant, which features two pigs playing guitars. Looking at these two cool pigs rocking out on their electric guitars created a narrative in my mind—these two pigs were welcoming me into the joint to eat their buddies who were, presumably, less cool? Less musically gifted? Smiles on their faces, wailing on their Stratocasters. Didn't they worry that they would be next?

It's been a very long time since I've eaten at a Red Hot & Blue restaurant, but I think about those pigs often. I think about how I am advertising my "coolness" and my talent, and if I'm inviting a level of harm as I do it.

When I think about the time and energy people have put into developing generative AI, and into understanding the impact of generative AI, I feel sad because we could have been working this hard on solving the labor issues that create a feeling of time crunching and disenfranchisement that generative AI purports to solve. We don't need AI agents; we need better work conditions so that we can use our expertise effectively. Generative AI is a bandage on real problems, and generative AI is always going to be the answer when the objective is to avoid disrupting capitalism. Solving higher education's labor problems may employ solutions that will not be the most late-capitalism friendly, but I think they would be the most humane-capitalism friendly. We talk about the attrition of students, the crisis of population that is leading higher education to some drastic austerity measures, and too often the solution is, frankly, to get rid of the people.

When we muse and fret over ways to increase enrollment, to reignite vibrant campus cultures that lead to the kind of student experience that enlivens learning, our kneejerk reaction should be to reject putting more screens and technology physically and emotionally between ourselves and students. We should be going heavier on creating opportunities for more authentic, interstitial interactions with educators of all kinds on campus, so students can benefit from the unique expertise offered by a vibrant and diverse higher education work force. The value of human interaction, where people have an opportunity to understand each other as complex individuals whose nonverbal behaviors are also instructive, needs to be brought to the fore again, but in a more inclusive and compassionate framework than has existed in the past.

Other industries are seeing similar threats posed by generative AI. A new company called Hippocratic AI "initially promoted a rate of $9 an hour for its AI assistants, compared with about $40 an hour for a registered nurse," reports Matthew Perrone (2025) for the *Associated Press.* Hippocratic AI dropped that sloganeering after pushback, but the threat remains, and nursing unions have been protesting over usage and protection for nurses from retaliation if they refuse to follow the automated bot's suggestions (Perrone 2025). In the employment sector, the City of New York enacted Local Law 144, which prohibits employers and employment agencies operating in New York City from using an "automated employment decision tool" unless the tool has been audited for bias in the last year, the results of said audit made available to the public, and employees and potential hires notified that such tools are being used in the hiring process. This law seems like a strong response to cases like HireVue, which I detailed in Chap. 3, as a third-party human resources agency that kept the problems with their use of generative AI in the hiring process out of sight. Of note, even when HireVue decided to take a more transparent approach, one of the solutions to expressed concerns about bias in hiring was that the company on whose behalf they were contracted to perform the hiring process would deploy human recruiters to interview potential candidates who eschewed HireVue's generative AI procedures. I thought immediately of the graduate students, who upon being given the breakout session information by the educator of record, lose an opportunity to practice that kind of class time preparation. Are human recruiters still going to be good at in-person interviews with neurotypical, let alone neurodiverse, candidates, if generative AI has taken over that task for the bulk of the initial interviewing process? The idea that "well, humans are bad at things, so we should have robots do those tasks, and when the robots mess up, the humans will save the day" falls apart quickly every time, because it seems like people either naturally or willfully forget how hard (or at least, time-consuming) it is to master tasks, not just learn how to do something passably. To master skills, it takes time, energy, commitment, and determination. Humans still need to learn to do things better, and they will not learn to do things better if they never have the time or incentive to learn.

Even HireVue acknowledges, in their transparency statement, that human transcription Word Error Rate (WER) is less than Rev. ai's WER (Rev.ai is the generative AI-powered transcription system). HireVue proffers, though, that "[...]it is neither economically feasible nor time-efficient to use human transcribers when processing the millions of interview responses so they can be auto-scored with our AI algorithms" (HireVue Explainability Statement). In modern parlance, that sounds like a *you* problem, HireVue and your customers. Why would hiring be treated so sloppily, as if it is a race to move bodies rather than find quality candidates who have the capacity to succeed and thrive, a process that necessarily takes time but would more likely contribute to a vibrant workplace?

And, sadly, even our current efforts to reign in bad actors is failing: as Roy Maurer (2024) reported for Society for Human Resource Management (SHRM), New York City Local Law 144 is essentially worthless as it comes with no enforceable consequences, and thus, employers are ignoring it. A good idea, conceivably, but if no one has the power to compel organizations to act in the prescribed manner, these laws are window dressing at best, anti-bias-washing at worst.

Conclusion

My sentiment here seems to be at the heart of what Ed Zitron calls "The Rot Economy" –as he diagnoses it, "Public and private investors, along with the markets themselves, have become entirely decoupled from the concept of what 'good' business truly is, focusing on one metric — one *truly noxious* metric — over all else: growth" (Zitron 2023). Growth without attention to expertise or learning from mistakes or developing people and products with a mind towards betterment, not numerical additions: this is the swirling cesspool in which we find ourselves. Through this lens, it makes sense why organizations are happy to blow right past opportunities to get it right when all they want to do is *get it*. One can see this in both the tech industry, where Zitron is focused, and in education—such is the explanation for why many institutions are focused on the acquisition of student bodies and the exploitation of adjuncts to provide a point person for the student bodies. That a critical mass of adjuncts represents people who are the most up to date on current research in their fields, as they are often graduate students and recent graduates, is a happy accident in the eyes of Upper Administration. It might even be considered a liability, in some cases, as those adjuncts may start feeling like their labor is wholly unrewarded by the employing institution. We are not creating situations where educators, full and part-time, can personally grow and thrive, taking the time to be continuous learners themselves in a manner that affords the time and brain-intensive work of slow, deep reading, and deeply conscious, iterative writing that develops both the thinker and the subsequent readers of the writing. We are hollowing out. Even institutions with large rosters of educators are creating situations, intentionally or unintentionally, that are draining the scholarly life right out of their employees. We may be here in the corporeal form, ready to teach the student bodies being chased down by officers of enrollment, but we are not being afforded opportunities to further our craft for ourselves and for others. Through retirements, firing, and the winnowing of part-time employees, soon our bodies will no longer be present either, save a few "core" educators who fire up the generative AI-run course shells and monitor the generative AI-content posted by the student bodies, to earn a certificate of passable-ness, ***ad infinitum***.

References

"AI Examples & Business Use Cases | IBM". (2024. February 14). https://www.ibm.com/think/topics/artificial-intelligence-business-use-cases

"AI Examples, Applications & Use Cases | IBM." n.d, March 24, 2025. https://www.ibm.com/think/topics/artificial-intelligence-business-use-cases.

Brenner, Sean. 2024. "Comparative Lit Class Will Be First in Humanities Division to Use UCLA-Developed AI System." UCLA, December 4. https://newsroom.ucla.edu/stories/comparative-literature-zrinka-stahuljak-artificial-intelligence.

Christie, Agatha. 2016. *And Then There Were None*. William Morrow.

"HireVue AI Explainability Statement." 2022. Hirevue.Com, March 31. https://www.hirevue.com/press-release/hirevue-launches-ai-explainability-statement-in-hr-industry-first.

June, Audrey Williams. 2023. "*How Do Humanities Majors Fare in the Work Force?*" The Chronicle of Higher Education, November 14. https://www.chronicle.com/article/how-do-humanities-majors-fare-in-the-work-force.

Maurer, Roy. 2024. *New York City AI Law is a Bust*. SHRM, February 18. https://www.shrm.org/topics-tools/news/technology/new-york-city-ai-law.

Palmer, Kathryn. 2025. *Publishers Embrace AI as Research Integrity Tool*. Inside Higher Ed, March 18. https://www.insidehighered.com/news/faculty-issues/research/2025/03/18/publishers-adopt-ai-tools-bolster-research-integrity.

Perrone, Matthew. 2025. *As AI Nurses Reshape Hospital Care, Human Nurses Push Back | AP News*. Associated Press. Accessed on March 16. https://apnews.com/article/artificial-intelligence-ai-nurses-hospitals-health-care-3e41c0a2768a3b4c5e002270cc2abe23.

Reuters, Thomson. 2024. "*Thomson Reuters Future of Professionals Report*." https://www.thomsonreuters.com/content/dam/ewp-m/documents/thomsonreuters/en/pdf/reports/future-of-professionals-report-2024.pdf.

Roberts, Jen. 2024. "*Using AI Tools to Give Feedback on High School Students' Writing*." Edutopia. Accessed on October 30, 2024. https://www.edutopia.org/article/ai-writing-feedback-students/.

Springsteen, Bruce. n.d. "Youngstown." Recorded June/July 2000 at Madison Square Garden, New York, NY. *YouTube video* 5:51. https://youtu.be/w038TQyWRN8?si=bWok-FBJogzYBfaU.

Suarez-Villa, Luis. 2012. *Globalization and Technocapitalism.* 1st ed. The Political Economy of Corporate Power and Technological Domination: Routledge. https://doi.org/10.4324/9781315585123.

Wang, Jenna. 2025. *NaNoWriMo No More? After a Series of Scandals, Some Iowans are Leaving the Nonprofit Writing Challenge Behind.* Little Village, March 11. http://littlevillagemag.com/nanowrimo-no-more/.

Zitron, Ed. 2023. "The Rot Economy." Ed Zitron's Where's Your Ed At, February 9. https://www.wheresyoured.at/the-rot-economy/.

CHAPTER 5

Sowers of Discord and Scandal: Generative AI and the Student/Educator Connection

Abstract This chapter is dedicated to teaching and will address pedagogy, but the primary focus when considering the impact of generative AI on the classroom is the discord sown between students and educators. Again, fractures in this critical relationship were visible long before fall of 2022, but the crisis of the COVID19 pandemic and the emergence of generative AI have turned a bad situation into a toxic one. We have an opportunity to course correct now in response to generative AI that could have long-lasting positive ramifications beyond the current AI discussion.

Keywords Teaching · Pedagogy · Generative AI

Introduction

In *The Divine Comedy*, Dante Alighieri gets positively gruesome when he paints a gory picture of the ninth *bolgia* in the eighth circle of Hell, where the "sowers of civic discord ('scandalo') and sowers of religious discord ('scisma')" reside (Barolini). The men who have created mortal conflict are themselves torn asunder by the demons of hell, just as they were responsible for tearing apart the fabric of the social and religious contracts within societies. The violence of the language indicates the severity of the

D. J. Gavin, *Generative AI and the Future of the Humanities*,
https://doi.org/10.1007/978-3-032-06534-6_5

crime—people who create harmful conflict for their own financial gain or power ascendency should be regarded as evildoers.

My initial reaction to the emergence of ChatGPT was centered around plagiarism, and I do not believe I was alone in that response. My understanding and feeling about the concept of plagiarism had evolved in my time as an English and composition educator. Where I had been draconian and punitive in my youth, I had started to reconceptualize my approach to composition pedagogy that I hoped would elicit the outcomes I wanted. The outcome I wanted was for students to demonstrate a command over their language and the effective communication of their thoughts. I wanted students to understand why it was important to cite sources correctly: to demonstrate how well they had researched their topic, how supported their ideas were by experts, and to give the reader the easiest way to find those sources if they wanted to read more. These factors fed into the establishment of the writer's ethos, and I wanted students to experience the weight of having to persuade the reader to take them seriously. I felt that emphasizing the "cheating" aspects of plagiarism reinforced a negative barrier between me and the students, setting up a scenario where they knew I was always on the lookout, like a sharpshooter, ready to penalize infractions.

I did not want to continue to build that barrier between myself and the students. The gulf between us seemed to be widening every year, especially in a class like first-year composition, where I was already a barrier, in most of my students' minds, to the "good stuff" in their majors—which were often not the humanities. Students are also participating in a world that expresses frustration and consternation with the skills the humanities are trying to impart, so they arrive at our classes with a feeling that their time is being wasted.

The "Value" of Grades

Every year, it seemed that students were growing more and more grade-driven—in some cases, it was due to educational opportunities like scholarships and awards, but those in turn came with grade point average price tags. Understandable, but I was unprepared for a student to approach me one day and say that they needed to earn a B+ or better in my first-year composition class to not only stay at the school but also stay in the United States. The situation put too much pressure on the student and the educator. I was flummoxed with that kind of pressure being put on me adjacently; yes, it was the responsibility of the student to meet my expectations, but we already know that grading is a flawed practice at best. The student had achieved a great thing, ostensibly: gaining entry into a good college. Yet it hung in the balance of a generally unfair system over which I had a modicum of control. I doubted that this student was going to enjoy my class, no matter how hard I tried, if they were constantly thinking about the precarity of their situation.

Grades enforce the greatest hierarchy in the classroom, but there are other things that separate us from students—students may have jobs, family commitments, or health concerns that prevent them from being fully present during the 50 or 75 minutes we have with them per class, if that class is in person. Even if you restrict the use of smartphones and laptops from your classroom, you are working with people (and likely yourself too) who have become acculturated to the reality of information at one's fingertips. We expect the pace of life to clip on at a certain measure, and when we try to enforce a collective slowing down, we should still anticipate challenges to that and resistance.

The COVID-19 pandemic put the most incredible physical distance between students and educators, as institutions in the United States and many other countries shut down and pivoted entirely to online instruction and services. It's important to remember that many educators at that time had little to no training in online education pedagogy. I felt fortunate that my community college pulled together a few of the trained faculty and staff and held impromptu workshops to bring us up to speed on some of the most important best practices of online delivery. I was grateful, but I also knew that a few training sessions did not make me the sort of expert who can maximize the online experience for the greatest number of people.

We emerged from the lockdowns of the pandemic to find a world more guarded and more distrustful than previously experienced. It's not just that some people want to tuck away behind a keyboard. That would be outlandishly straight-forward. Many people prefer to experience the world with the extension of the smartphone in hand. We've seen images of people recording concerts with their smartphones, as opposed to listening and dancing. That mediated distance—meant to capture the moment in something more permanent than the mind, but at what sacrifice?—gets replicated in other ways, including the classroom.

There are many ways in which technology can improve the educational experience for students, including online learning. There are students whose needs are met with good online learning pedagogy, and they are able to thrive—I would never want to undo the progress we have made in terms of accessibility for all students, especially those with conditions that would otherwise keep them disenfranchised from an education. In general, I think an LMS, when operated effectively and thoughtfully, can offer a level of consistency across the curriculum and student services that can lower barriers. Too often, however, it seems that these technologies wind up creating barriers, consuming the educator's time (either because of their own knowledge gaps regarding the LMS, or because they are trying to incorporate way too many bells and whistles in hopes of capturing students' attentions) or the student's time (a learning curve in terms of using the LMS, a incongruent experience due to a differing in LMS quality across classes and departments, and/or a lack of access to equipment or a stable internet connection). Faculty would protest, rightly so, that they do not have time to become masters of their institution's LMS, especially when institutions may change their LMS to keep up with emerging technologies. We expect faculty to be experts in their disciplines, which rarely to never include LMS. We could expect faculty who know they will be teaching online courses to become experts in that pedagogy, but again, there seems to be a lack of time, as I discussed in greater detail in Chap. 4. Whether there truly is a lack of time, or just a perception of a time deficit, the fact seems to stand that educators feel pulled in too many directions to master other subjects other than their disciplinary focus. And even then, how many faculty feel that they can stay abreast of all the disciplinary evolutions that occur in their field?

These questions seem connected to a false perception that the younger generations are hopelessly addicted to the newest technology and, critically, that they are "digital natives." The reasoning seems to be that if we just "meet the students where they are," in terms of technology, we will win them over. We will make learning so much easier that they will simply have to learn. Everything will be digital, and it will be attractive and easy to navigate. Surely, then, the learning will occur.

It's easy to make assumptions, I think, as we see a world around us with smartphones in hands at all times. Most people pull out tablets and laptops mindlessly when sitting down in class or to work in writing centers. People, especially young people, seem to move through this digital world easily. And they do, with the technology they like. Most young people understand how to use TikTok and Instagram effortlessly.

They might be able to shop on Poshmark and communicate via WhatsApp as if it was second nature.

Ask these students to format a Microsoft Word document, or upload a file to an LMS, and you might find a very different level of confidence. From my vantage point, if a task cannot be done easily on a smartphone, young people are less likely to have prior knowledge of how to execute the task. Some students only have smartphones with which to work, and so they are limited even further, as they are only able to take advantage of desktop computers when on campus. In this way, there is great overlap between much older students and much younger students—both may find using the LMS to be another literacy that is foreign to them. Whatever technology they remember from high school does not prepare them for the LMS we use today. Too often, faculty are either unable or unavailable to tutor students in the necessary LMS literacy that keeps them at a distance from the classwork they need, including assignment instructions, syllabi and schedules, and places to upload work. In my experience, they make use of places like writing centers and other student service centers, sitting with us and making sense of it together. We can form connections with students, for which I am grateful, but we also see the frustration that can lead to problems. Some institutions work LMS literacy into their first-year experiences, or into orientation programs, but that may not be sufficient for all students.

The Specter of Plagiarism

The other, more sinister way we put technology in between the educator and the student is through surveillance protocols. The is nothing new, again—for decades, we have surveilled students by having them complete timed essays in class with only a writing utensil and paper. As we learned how many students were excluded from success when we used such surveillance methods, we continued to surveil in this way but carved out exceptions for students who needed accommodations due to mental and physical health. For decades too, we have employed plagiarism detection software, most often Turnitin.com, to screen student papers for cheating. Students were often required to consent to have their paper screened—most students, and many educators, were unaware that students were also consenting to have their work stored in large databases, which built out Turnitin.com's ability to sell its services as fool-proof. Those of us who teach using writing assessments have spent untold hours of our lives talking about plagiarism and attempting to catch plagiarism.

The emergence of ChatGPT in Fall 2022 took this obsession and threw it into overdrive, and it was understandable. Suddenly, everyone had access to a program that could generate passable writing from whole cloth. No student, would ever submit self-derived work ever again. Worse still, established plagiarism detectors were unable to discern generated text from an LLM, leaving educators with no defense against the tidal wave of machine writing.

Educators now had to get up to speed with an unfamiliar technology with little to no help from said technology developers, save a few inert warnings that students should not use said technology to cheat. As soon as we found ChatGPT in our laps, those same developers and other aspirational entrepreneurs declared they had programs that could detect generative AI in student writing. And so, educators flocked to these promises in the form of GPTZero and Turnitin's own AI "detector," feeling as if the "problem" had been solved. No matter how many plagiarism tips and tricks students were learning on TikTok—now we had them in our sights!

This technology life cycle has been galling to watch and experience. Generative AI, using LLMs, seems to fly in the face of everything the humanities hold dear: the nature of human thought, the dedicated research and vetting of said research, the power of composition to help a person arrive at clarity of thought, and such. I am not suggesting that developers such as Altman owe educators any consideration, but I am suggesting that it tracks that Silicon Valley would be uniquely disinterested in considering the implications of their work on the critical humanities skills people need to survive and thrive in a capitalistic democracy. That they would drop a cluster bomb like generative AI into our laps, and then "innovate" terrible products to "fix" the problems they created is, simply, insult to injury. AI detectors are unreliable but are presented as entirely reliable. Read the fine print, and we learn that these detectors are in no way foolproof, and that the developers recommend educators use them as "conversation starters" with students they suspect of using AI. Yet, by this point, the educator has potentially lost the battle precisely because it has been set up as a battle.

Pedagogy built on adversarial positioning can lead to good outcomes for some, but we know that it is not the best approach for many students. We have a more diverse student body, deliberately—we've worked very hard at making higher education more available to a wider body of learners. In part, that is surely work built on the principles of justice and equity: higher education cannot just be the province of wealthy white young Protestant men, as it was prior to the 1950s, before social movements and the GI Bill (which gave veterans financial coverage for college) in the United States. We have worked to outlaw desegregation and access inequality as a moral good. It is also true that higher education is run as a business, and more students equals more revenue. That is particularly true today in the United States, as we are experiencing a population atrophy– high school students are simply not as plentiful in many areas of the country as they once were. If we the institution are not attracting an incredibly diverse body of students, we will fail to survive as an organization.

An adversarial relationship between educator and student, in a classical model, has been promoted in the media as a negative (think Terence Fletcher in *Whiplash*, Jerry Hathaway in *Real Genius*, and Gale Nolan in *Dead Poets Society*). In reality, many educators reminisce about the severe hierarchy they experienced in their educational lineage and long for the days of "sage on the stage" and draconian punishments. The most telling evidence of this resistance is the occasional kneejerk response to generative AI, where some educators seemed committed to rolling back Universal Design for Learning (UDL) principles and accommodations for students—all the best practices we have innovated and pushed for adoption just right out the window in favor of "blue book and pencil," because nothing could be more important than eliminating cheating. That reaction indicates that, at its heart, the primary function of learning for many educators is domination through penalty. If grades are the only currency, then we must create a compliant culture through physical situations of austerity. This may create a positive experience for some students, but certainly not for all. And the educator finds themself consumed with adopting a pugilistic stance, which likely does not promote professional growth that disciplines demand.

Rigor as Value

We've been having these kinds of pedagogical fights for decades. We've talked about flipped classrooms, emphasizing process over product, and even ungrading principles. Through the State University of New York (SUNY) system, we are offered free courses that help educators not only understand but implement the principles of UDL. I can understand how some of these ideas appear to fly in the face of the concept of rigor and thus seem to be watering down the quality of instruction. We lament how students cannot read long novels and cannot write 30-page essays, as we did in our undergraduate, graduate, and post-graduate careers. Maybe we should do a better job of interrogating the idea of rigor, and see if "rigor" should be rehabilitated to more accurately reflect the needs of the students we are charged with educating? Thinking about "rigor" as "stiffness," as in rigor mortis, seems to have much in common with how we use rigor these days. Is there sufficient rigidity and adherence to the historical ways of doing things? Do we have enough inflexibility to properly train students for … the workforce? Graduate studies? Have we put enough gate-keeping measures in place so that only the most deserving students can progress through to the next level?

I would prefer to think about rigor as an attention to thoroughness and accuracy, which entails that I, as the educator, constantly reevaluate to what skills and abilities "thoroughness and accuracy" should relate, as well as the best strategies to lead students towards mastery. For many, many years, I required a lengthy research paper at the end of the semester for first-year composition. Students struggled, and I routinely wondered if they were struggling over the skills that were really most important to me, or struggling over time management, for example, which was not a skill I was focused on teaching in the classroom. I felt that a key part of the student experience was to learn those skills—time management, reading scholarly articles, and seeking out support from other academic services like writing centers and libraries as part of the necessary labor of student suffering. No English professor in my experience had ever broken down those steps—I was expected to go suss it out for myself. I believed that sussing out period was critical for other students. When a librarian colleague challenged me on why I was asking students to do this long research paper, I balked. They needed to experience the patience and commitment to the process that is necessary for deep thinking and learning, I argued. And yet, was it really a page number that was the indicator of patience, commitment, and learning? Or was I creating an arbitrary hurdle because I had the same hurdles placed in front of me? Was long-form research writing the best way to have students practice the skills I believed critically important, when that form was not likely to be useful to them in their daily lives? My answers to these questions necessitated a change in my pedagogy because I was not getting students any step closer to the essential skills through an opaque and antiquated method.

Process-Oriented Pedagogy: Suggestions for Practice

What does a pedagogy that rewards the process, and not the product, look like? I am certain many expert educators have numerous examples, but I will suggest a few practical ideas that could be customized for writing-focused courses. One element that is necessary and out of our control, in most cases, is a small class roster; fewer than 20 is optimal. A small class means that the educator is physically able to have deeper connections, to speak directly to students about what interests them and help them make meaning through our disciplines. If you are unable to control class size, creating small groups within your larger group can be helpful. Students should be afforded opportunities to engage in conversation about the material they are reading, including their approaches to reading, their struggles with reading, and how they go about solving their challenges with reading. In my experience, students are not necessarily aware of the process of solving conflict in the learning process, and, more importantly, the necessity of solving conflicts in the learning process instead of avoiding them. Take time during class to practice reading with an attention to the process of looking up words, taking notes, investigating ideas that are foreign to the reader with an eye towards reliable sources of information (for example, avoiding the generative AI summaries at the top of Google's search engine page). As Wolfe (2019) wrote, "Reading, at least all deep reading, requires the use of analogical reasoning and inference if we are to uncover the multiple layers of meaning in what we read" (59). If students have not practiced analogical reasoning and inference skills, they will need to see you model them, and they will need to practice them in your presence, with the camaraderie of their peers. Demonstrate your process for reading and include an explanation of how you find time for reading, what sacrifices you make to find time to read, and why you make those sacrifices. Tell them what it was like for you to be an undergraduate, even if you felt like these skills came easily for you. Talk about your process of being a student scholar and give your students an opportunity to model your behavior and create their own scholarly processes.

In fact, have them memorialize these processes by writing them down. I do not mean reading journals based on the material they have for class—I mean the process by which they find time to read, when they read, what they do when they come across a word that is unknown to them, or a difficult concept. If they include thoughts about the concepts they understand, fantastic, but the most important part of an entry level skills assessment should be the demonstration of scholarly practices. This kind of journaling can be continued when your class pedagogy turns to writing assessments—ask students to memorialize their process. Are they morning writers or evening writers? Late night writers by choice or by necessity? What is their preferred environment in which to write: quiet, with music, with low-level bustling in a coffee shop? Do they ever feel like they are actively choosing their writing environment, or are they having to make compromises that impact the quality of the work they deliver to you?

Ask students to include the habits, practices, and knowledge that they bring with them to your class. For example, students may come to your class with a habit of outlining. Ask them to share with the class why they have that habit, and if they find that it works well for them or not. Ask students to talk about where they get information, and when they say "nowhere," ask them what kind of media they consume. Ask them to keep a media contact diary, or, put another way, ask them to keep a detailed list of everything they see on their smartphones for a week. Everything, especially the ads. Talk about what content relates to your course, directly or, more likely, indirectly. Ask students about their hobbies and their extracurricular pursuits. Ask them how they dedicate themselves to practicing a sport, for example. Point out where they might be modeling for themselves the kind of skills that will make them strong critical readers and writers. Ask them to write all of this down after they have discussed these things aloud—here is where, if you have a large class, you can make use of small groups where students can feel heard by a few instead of trying to speak to the mass. Students who feel nervous about speaking extemporaneously can be encouraged to write their ideas first and then share.

Read these records of their intellectual lives with an eye towards their process, not the content of their writing or the elegance of their prose. When you spy anything that suggests a good habit, point it out, regardless of what the context is. Look for moments of critical thinking or logical reasoning, and point them out enthusiastically, even if they are related to an episode of *Buffy the Vampire Slayer*. *Especially* if it is related to *Buffy the Vampire Slayer*, because that student may feel like they have gone out on a limb to disclose an "unscholarly" interest. It feels good to have the things we do acknowledged, especially when we are not expecting it.

Be generous with your praise and repeatedly—more than you think you should—tie these habits back to the academic work you are asking the students to do. Demonstrate that so many of these habits relate to habits they are already exhibiting. Share your habits, including the ones you do not like and are working to change. Model for those around you the way to be a continuous student of life and of oneself.

As you plan your class pedagogy, look for ways to have students capture this information from their lives in a written form that is rewarded through points towards their grades. At least at the moment, we still live in a world where academic grading trumps goodwill and healthy learning practices. Even if we incorporate elements of "ungrading" into our pedagogy, grades are the currency through which internal and external forces determine student worth. Your grade scheme is your statement of values, and you have the opportunity to make choices that telegraph directly to the student what you value most. If you want students to dig into the trenches of writing, that messy, human work of creating and preserving thought, jettison high-stakes, single iterative writing assignments. Put your points where your mouth is—if you tell students that you are more interested in their messy processes and the way they get to their ideas, spread the bulk of your grade points across iterative, informal operations-focused reflective writing. Accord more points to the students' descriptions of their writing process, and analysis of the efficacy of their work based on your assessment rubric, rather than the finished paper. Make their metacommentary the primary assessment object, rather than the final draft, and you may see students who are learning to be scholars through the practice of scholarship, not people who can turn in a paper.

Conclusion

I understand that the pedagogy I am describing demands an incredible amount of time and effort, as I addressed in Chap. 4. I am presenting what I think would bring us closer to a platonic ideal, that would bring us back to the essential skills valued by the humanities that are critical to being a human. I hope that these are the practices that begin to turn the ship that is sailing into illiteracy and Narcissus' numbness. I think about what Wolfe (2019) warned, "Absent the checks and balances provided by both our prior knowledge content and our analytical processes, we run the risk of digesting information without questioning whether [...] [it] is accurate and free from external motivations and prejudices" (57).

When we ask students to be scholars of their scholarly journey through journaling and informal writing, we are also inviting them to record the chaotic process of acquiring knowledge, and give them a commemorative place to review the successes and challenges as they continue on. We can "go back to the basics," not punitively (such as forcing students to hand write essays in class), but as an evolution: we have an opportunity to teach and inspire student writers to develop an inquiry process, and we can support their efforts to clearly explain the unique and beautiful way only their mind can process the texts that surround them. This practice is an opportunity for students, and us, to validate why the work is hard and because it is hard, valuable as our minds evolve. Only through that evolution do we have any chance to battle forth through the rot and slop littering the path towards actualization.

References

Barolini, Teodolinda. 2018. "Inferno 28: Tuscany's evil seed." Commento Baroliniano, Digital Dante. Columbia University Libraries. https://digitaldante.columbia.edu/dante/divine-comedy/inferno/inferno-28/

Wolfe, Maryanne. 2019. *Reader*. Come Home: The Reading Brain in a Digital World. Harper.

CHAPTER 6

Deep, Deliberate Engagement: The Way Forward is Through

Abstract This final chapter argues that we should use our hard-won skills, developed through our humanistic work, to take the problem of incapacitating technocapitalism head on. Whether or not generative AI is a sustainable product from a sustainable industry, we have critical work to do to instigate a public reckoning around the value of critical reading and writing. We cannot continue to cede ground on this issue of what people need to survive and thrive, and we must endeavor to forge new alliances through deepening network ties with ostensible comrades in public-facing industries.

Keywords Reading · Writing · Generative AI

Introduction

Let us end here, then, with a reference to celebrated American poet Robert Frost's 1915 poem, "A Servant to Servants." The speaker is a woman tasked with serving scores of men who come live on the property she shares with her husband, Len. She expresses her sadness and frustration with her lot in life: "There's nothing but a voice-like left inside/ That seems to tell me how I ought to feel, / And would feel if I wasn't all gone wrong" (Frost 1917, 64). She labors for these men, whom she

D. J. Gavin, *Generative AI and the Future of the Humanities*, https://doi.org/10.1007/978-3-032-06534-6_6

notes have incredible freedom to come and go from the beautiful lakeside home where she is ostensibly trapped. She complains about the boarders she must tend to:

> We have four here to board, great good-for-nothings,
> Sprawling about the kitchen with their talk
> While I fry their bacon. Much they care!
> No more put out in what they do or say
> Than if I wasn't in the room at all. (Frost 1917, 67)

I feel profound sympathy for this woman and her situation; as a woman of no financial means in America in 1915, this nameless woman was bound to serve her husband's interests, and if that meant providing all the care to lodgers on her own, so be it. As she describes laboring for people who do not seem to care for either her work or her very presence in the room, I also hear echoes of what educators are experiencing today. When the great pivot to online learning happened in the spring and fall of 2020, many educators who had never been required to teach online scrambled to quickly learn best practices and create as positive an experience as possible for students. There has been much written and discussed regarding learning loss due to the lockdowns in the U.S., for example, while little time has been spent acknowledging the work most educators did, let alone acknowledging that online teaching has a pedagogy all its own. That disregard was painful, but so too was the dreaded black Zoom screen boxes that many of us faced in those semesters—of the students who did show up for our now-online courses, how many turned their cameras on? How many tried to talk with us as we struggled to mimic the pedagogy we planned for inside the classroom?

And of course, let's live in truth: student engagement was a serious topic of conversation long before COVID-19 descended upon us. We have been discussing and modifying our approaches to pedagogy for decades, trying to find the right alchemy of pressure and inspiration to have students show up to class having done the homework, ready to engage in fruitful discussions. This work has long been on the fore of our minds, with good reason: Naiditch (2010) argues, "Schools empower learners toward participation and action by teaching them how to listen, how to identify alternatives, how to consider possibilities and how to search for multiple possible answers" (95). We must engage and teach students in humanities-centered skills because they are learning require these fundamental skills to survive a world that is increasingly anti-humanistic.

Deep, Deliberate Engagement

Now, we are all mostly back in classrooms, attempting to battle with an addiction to smartphones, general distractions including the necessity for many students to work full-time while they pursue their studies, and those who have domestic responsibilities to families and friends in need. There are many valid reasons why students find it difficult to show up to our classes having done the homework, understood the homework, and ready to engage with us in fulsome discussions. Setting aside the validity, this leaves educators in an existential lurch. Many of us go into classrooms trying to fry the bacon, while we are lucky if 51% of the students enter the classroom, much less do anything other than sprawl about the classroom, earbuds in, phones to noses. We are challenged physically, emotionally, professionally, and personally, and that is taxing. Those feelings are real and need to be acknowledged in more than just empty platitudes.

In fact, acknowledging the current strain on educators is part of the strategy I would propose to move forward. The speaker in "A Servant and Servants" states, "It's rest I want—there, I have said it out— [...] from doing/ Things over and over that just won't stay done" (Frost 1917, 66). The idea of the work never been fully realized resonates with me as I think of educators who are deep into their careers, who want to believe that their pedagogy is the one true way to teach students. I am not suggesting that humanities educators should be exempt from continuously learning and revising their pedagogy—I am suggesting that when it seems like the techno-late-stage-capitalism is against the very skills you treasure, you balk a bit at being asked to change yourself instead of changing the techno-late-stage-capitalism.

Here we are, though, and the speaker repeats something her husband Len has said to her: "He says the best way out is always through. / And I agree to that, or in so far/ As that I can see no way out but through—" (Frost 1917, 66). There's a notable difference, where Len believes it is the best way, the speaker says she can see no other way. The speaker has few options: continue her work, hoping for some gratitude and rest; educators have the option to quit academia, and many have. Other educators who rely on written assessments have taken the ostrich approach: if we just pretend like ChatGPT isn't out there and just march onward in willful ignorance as we have in decades past, everything will be alright in the end. As discussed in previous chapters, that is simply a disastrous approach. We must deal with the world as it is, not as we wish it would be.

If we agree that the humanities are vital to the success of the person, the community, and the world, then we cannot give up trying to teach these skills. We must press forward with an updated version of teaching critical thinking skills that reflects a ChatGPT-infused reality (which is also infused with many other threats to critical thinking, such as the destruction of local news organizations and the proliferation of misinformation in viral settings). We must not do this piecemeal, however, and we cannot rely on the old structures of information dissemination either. Our research on these topics can't be hidden behind paywalls or require R1 institutional access to read them. We have to change our approach to teaching pedagogy and making pedagogy review a natural part of the profession. We need to rethink the way we use the term "academic freedom," and make sure we are not allowing that concept to be weaponized as a shield against necessary changes to our teaching methods. It should not be controversial to expect educators to continue their education and require them to at least acknowledge the world in which we are forced to live.

What does that look like in practice? It should not be beyond the pale to require educators to, at minimum, understand generally what generative AI is and can do, to be aware of what generative AI may look like in the non-academic world (especially as it might relate to one's discipline), and to provide students with a clear understanding of what generative AI use is permitted and what is not permitted. I can certainly see how some predict that the AI bubble will burst sooner than later, but the timing of the burst matters not at all with respect to how we need to change our approach to teaching and learning. Essentially, we have to talk about how we got to a place where writing, reading, and critically thinking were so heinously devalued that people would sink billions of dollars into making sure people could avoid those activities for the rest of their lives under the guise of "saving time." These enormous research questions should be the focus for a significant portion of us because we will find ourselves on defense forever going forward. ChatGPT and generative AI are a symptom of a much greater problem, and that problem will not be eradicated if, tomorrow, big tech companies like NVIDIA and OPENAI are put to pasture.

This is why I rather wantonly reworded Frost's beautiful poetry, to change the word "out" to "forward." I do not believe there is an "out" here, not if we do agree that reading, writing, and critical thinking are indispensable attributes of healthy, happy people. We are obligated to press forward, not hit the eject button. We cannot simply white-knuckle this moment, because the next upheaval will be on its heels. We have to have a heart-to-heart with the elephant in the room and ask clear and hard questions about how the poor elephant came to be stuck in the room in the first place. The work will be challenging, but it will be our greatest defense against future assaults.

What does this kind of transformational work look like? I would argue we have to form more effective networks of communication, because I think people are already proposing great ideas for revolutionizing pedagogy. Educators do not have effective communication threads to disseminate and activate new ideas within our incredibly diverse professional communities. We will have to think about doing away with prejudices about who teaches what and where and dispose of gatekeeping efforts that keep the "elites" from discourse with the "scrum" (I cheerfully count myself as scrum here, to be clear!). We should consider the K-12 educators in the humanities courses as our brethren, and engage with them more materially (by that, I mean having summer-time round tables and professional development opportunities to learn from each other). As someone who teaches English courses in higher education, I am dependent on the work done by my colleagues during these students' formative years. Why wouldn't I be passionately invested in the work they are doing, and the challenges they may be facing?

We could look for grounds for consensus more aggressively, even just at the level of knowing people must learn to read, write, and think critically. Even if we diverge on if and when generative AI should come into the pedagogical mix, we should all be able to agree that people must be able to read, write, and think critically on their own first, with limited and necessary accommodations for those with disabilities, before we accept the intrusion of chatbots.

We likely diverge on the ways we teach, the explanations we give students about why we are teaching what we teach and how we teach it, and even if those explanations are necessary. I think about the many discussions I had while working part-time at a private "liberal arts" college that has a thriving business school. Students flocked to the business program and grumbled about their humanities requirements (as did some of their professors). The humanities professors were frustrated and angry that they were seeing their number of students declared as majors crater and felt disrespected by their colleagues. These humanities folks lamented the need to convince students that the humanities were important, though many also did not want to verbalize the idea that the humanities could be linked to the mass production of worker cogs. I appreciated their dilemma, to a point. I think about Sherlock Holmes, who took such great pleasure in his work that he often eschewed credit and sometimes payment; in "The Adventure of the Norwood Builder," he refuses Inspector Lestrade's offer to include Holmes' name in his report, saying, "'Not at all. The work is its own reward'" (Doyle 1903, 495). I imagine that many people in the humanities feel somewhat similarly, that the acquisition of knowledge is, unto itself, a fulfilling pursuit, as it brings people closer to a state of self-actualization. I agree wholeheartedly with the spirit of this entreaty. The idea of an institution of learning becoming a factory that pumps out worker cogs is an anathema to many of us. Education is romanticized to have life-altering possibilities and to envision our institutions as servants to the Capitalism God is offensive. I am not suggesting we fall in line and support the Churn Factory concept, but I think it is time to revisit how we can more effectively present a vision to people of what we can offer them. Business schools do not have to think in these terms (though I am confident that they, too, are experiencing the same general pressures we all are, in terms of student population attrition due to demographic changes, as well as government funding crises that affect every department). Western culture speaks clearly and convincingly that business is Real, jobs are Real, and money is Real; everything else is Abstraction. The rise of grifters and influencer culture means that people are looking at every interest or idea through the lens of profitability. Hobbies like writing fan fiction or craft-making are coupled with the language of monetization. The thinking seems to go, if you are going to put time and energy into an activity, especially an activity you enjoy, you should work towards compensation for every expenditure of time and energy. This may be tied to the canard, "Find a job you love, and you'll never work a day in your life." Doing something for its own sake is not part of the grind culture mentality, and I think we need to consider strategies for piercing through that grind culture veil.

There is a flip side to grind culture, too, which many people teaching today recognize: a pervasive vibe of numbness. To me, it is not apathy; it is a feeling of being so bombarded by messages, spoken and unspoken, that a person cannot (or will not) engage with their environment in meaningful ways. In the United States, people have generally grown up with some idea of an abstract American Dream which is defined by capitalism. We have been told that if we work hard enough, we will have financial wealth, and that wealth will look like a nice house, primarily. We will have enough money to enjoy vacations and give our children a better life than the one we had growing up. Those people who are inherently good and hard-working (the two must always go together) will receive the cash windfall they so obviously deserve. The reality of a post-2008 world in the United State, however, does not (and cannot) afford many people this fantasy. Following the financial crisis and the resulting Great Recession, homeownership was at one of the highest recorded rates from 2005 to 2007, at about 66 to 67 percent of the population. In 2010, that percentage was down to 65.4 percent. By 2015, it cratered to 63 percent. In 2019, the numbers showed a slight improvement to 64.1 percent, and that year is the last recorded in the "Homeownership in the United States: 2005 to 2019" report (Mateyka and Mazur 2021, 1–2). In the wake of the COVID-19 pandemic, the United States has experienced a further challenging housing crisis, among other inflationary crises that impact most people.

In the wake of this reality, the great promise of hard work and clean living is moot. Some still cling to the "rise and grind" mentality, but it seems like more and more people are sliding into the numbness. What a perfect spell for generative AI to emerge, when people feel less like thinking and working, when there seems no point to any of it.

To the educators, who feel like nothing we do penetrates, who feel like the culture and the politicians in power are against us, who feel like our own institutional upper administrations barely give lip service to valuing the work we do—why should we be the only ones who "beat on, boats against the current, borne back ceaselessly into the past" (Fitzgerald 1986, 182)? Why shouldn't we purchase an AI essay grading tool and let the robots grade the robots?

Our commitment to the work cannot continue to take on the flavor of a vocation or a calling. That framing has led us, in part, to this moment; it is too easy to be manipulated, abused, and be battered into using victim-centered terminology to describe our situation. If we truly understand our value, we need to come up with better ways to communicate that value, in terms that project strength, fearlessness, and command of the material realities. We cannot change the nature of the American Dream, but we can demonstrate the way in which the humanities can change the way people can experience a dream for the future that is based on truth and personal agency.

Not Alone, But Together

We must acknowledge that, to make these changes, we will have to do incredible amounts of work that goes beyond the work we are contracted to do. I try to never lose sight of the fact that the work we do in the classrooms and in all learning spaces is plenty enough just as it is, and yet, I believe we have to find a way to do labor outside of that. I believe that one part of the strategy needs to be building coalitions and partnerships with potentially unlikely allies, as a way of lessening the load on any one group.

First, we must unionize. As I write this book in March 2025, I am currently serving on my union's negotiating team during our contract campaign, while, separately, we are currently being asked to weigh in on using generative AI tutor bots produced by SUNY. The pressure to defend and honor our labor inside and outside of the classroom is extreme, especially when we are facing systemic threats from the statewide apparatus. I imagine many readers are nodding along at this point, and if you feel as pressured as I do, we must leverage our strength into unions and then form clear communication lines across local, state, and national unions. That work is already happening—in my case, my campus union recently voted to affiliate with the American Association of University Professors (AAUP), who had already joined forces with American Federation of Teachers (AFT), New York State United Teachers (NYSUT), National Education Association (NEA), and American Federation of Labor and Congress of Industrial Organizations (AFL-CIO), which is the largest federation of unions in the United States. These larger organizations have access to more of everything, and as a member organization, we can share in the largesse of legal and advocacy information. If your campus is not unionized, start investigating the possibilities. If you are unionized, seek more opportunities to affiliate with state and national unions, as well as unions that are not strictly bound up in education—other unions may well support our causes and be willing to stand together in a fight for more opportunities to create deep learning in resistance to labor threats at large.

We need to find allies in unlikely media sources and in politics. This means putting ourselves out in potentially unfamiliar and less enjoyable situations but needs must. To be sure, we face a difficult front on both lines. We can see how traditional mainstream media's power is dissolving (by mainstream, I mean network news stations, radio, and the major newspapers of record). We need to be realistic, here, that some people and industries may not be as keen on improving critical literacy skills as we may wish them to be. Maybe we do not have the same kind of threat to literacy as Frederick Douglass faced as an enslaved man, but we do have examples of why a highly literate populace is a potential threat to the power and wealth of others. Take Facebook as a ripe example: a highly literate populace might be less susceptible to an algorithm designed to ensnare through hate, as hate must be artificially sustained through emotion and illogic. A critically literate person may organically spend less time on social media because it is precisely *not* deep reading and deep thinking and cannot sustain deep writing and deep personal bonding. A critically literate person may start moving much slower than the captains of industry may like, and that radical yet essential slowing down may prove to be a pain point in terms of forming alliances.

For example, we are seeing media companies cede their agency to OpenAI: most recently to fall in is Guardian Media Group (GNM Press Office 2025), which announced a "strategic partnership" with OpenAI in February 2025. There is mounting pressure to make generative AI a part of every facet of life, and industries are likely to balk at being asked to support a tempering of those capitalistic fires, let alone helping usher in a moratorium that gives people time and space to cultivate the kind of deep critical literacy skills we know are necessary to survive, let alone thrive, in this rot-y, grift-y future. That does not mean we should not try—we should look for complementary yet edgy spaces where interested parties may lie. It means creating new avenues for conversations about critical literacy that do not feel heavy-handed or overbearing. We must identify like-minded people in the developer sphere who are interested in partnering with us on these new channels for communication and share our commitment to open access and transparency.

We must also seek to partner with law makers who are in agreement with the core values we hold with respect to human authority and agency, rather than politicians who either seek to profit from generative AI or who are content to proffer toothless legislation like New York Local Law 144.

In March 2025, a promising bill called the "New York Workforce Stabilization Act," sponsored by New York State Senator Michelle Hinchey, is languishing in the New York State Senate's Labor Committee. This bill appears to have the sort of teeth that Local Law 144 lacks, as it acts to amend state labor law to require certain businesses to audit artificial intelligence impacts to their work force and then, critically, amends the tax law to levy a surcharge on business that use artificial intelligence or data mining or have more than fifteen employees negatively impacted by the use of AI. Whether this bill will make it out of the committee intact, or even at all, remains to be seen, but requiring compliance with transparency through financial disincentives seems like it puts the laborer as the priority.

We have examples of walking this "broligarchy" back, never forget. One resonant resent example features the proliferation of larger and larger touch pad screens for high end automobiles in lieu of knobs and buttons. The thinking seemed to be that touch screens looked fancier and more modern, and knobs looked old fashioned. Presumably, designers felt that there was more efficiency to be had by putting essential functions all on one touch screen, but they were quite mistaken. The Swedish automotive magazine *Vi Bilägare* reported on testing they performed on eleven modern vehicles, where drivers attempted to perform four different essential tasks while driving, such as turning on the headlights. They reported that "Tesla gets a special mention for the egregious migration of even the windshield wipers to the central touchscreen [and...] [t]he driver in the BMW iX took almost a kilometre to perform all tasks" (Semler and Affat 2024).

Fortunately, the European New Car Assessment Programme (Euro NCAP), which is a voluntary car safety performance assessment programme and "the peak body for assessing new car safety," according to Mulach (2024), had been paying attention. Euro NCAP and its counterpart, Australasian New Car Assessment Program (ANCAP) have gone on record urging manufacturers to return to physical buttons and knobs for critical functions "to enhance driver safety by minimizing distractions caused by touchscreens" (Alcomendas 2024). They are going even further than suggestions: Euro NCAP will introduce new rules in January 2026 that will penalize new vehicles with certain critical functions that are embedded in the console touchpad instead of being controlled by physical instruments (Mulach 2024).

Bender et al. (2021) lay out a plan for the way LLM developers might see a path forward to join the humanities in a quest to return to a critical literacy focus. They argue that developers can find inspiration in the educational movement to "decolonize," where many disciplines, especially in the humanities, interrogated our traditional objects of study with an eye towards the pervasiveness of white colonizer texts. Bender et al. (2021) suggest a similar tactic, advocating for a strategy to move "[...] towards oral histories due to the overrepresentation of colonial views in text, and curate training datasets through a thoughtful process of deciding what to put in, rather than aiming solely for scale and trying haphazardly to weed out, post-hoc, flotsam deemed 'dangerous', 'unintelligible', or 'otherwise bad'" (614). We can be wise and strategic, moving slowly and breaking less, so that we do not sacrifice opportunities to improve critical literacies for those who could uniquely benefit from LLM technology, rather than tie ourselves in knots trying to find a plausible use case for billionaires who have no investment in the material well-being of those who are compelled to serve their data-selves on platters at their altar.

Conclusion

An action step today, every day, would be for each of us to adopt mindful practices in our own lives and then talk about our processes relentlessly. Let everyone in our lives know what we are doing to read and write deeply. Let people know when you have failed, and when you are picking yourself back up again. Expose your cowardice and your bravery and ask others to do the same. Speak and write at length about why literacy is the path to freedom and self-actualization. Be bold and go deep, because others will follow.

References

Alcomendas, Anby. 2024. "EURO NCAP, ANCAP Encourage Physical Buttons for Vehicle Safety." *AfMA* (blog). March 12. https://afma.org.au/euro-ncap-ancap-encourage-physical-buttons-for-vehicle-safety/.

Bender, Emily M., Timnit Gebru, Angelina McMillan-Major, and Shmargaret Shmitchell. 2021. "On the Dangers of Stochastic Parrots: Can Language Models Be Too Big?" In *Proceedings of the 2021 ACM Conference on Fairness, Accountability, and Transparency*, 610–623. FAccT '21. New York, NY:

Association for Computing Machinery. https://doi.org/10.1145/3442188.3445922.

Doyle, Arthur Conan. 1903. "The Return of Sherlock Holmes: The Adventure of the Norwood Builder." *Strand Magazine: An Illustrated Monthly* 26 (155).

Finkenstaedt-Quinn, Solaire A., Michael Petterson, Anne Gere, and Ginger Shultz. 2021. "Praxis of Writing-to-Learn: A Model for the Design and Propagation of Writing-to-Learn in STEM." *Journal of Chemical Education* 98 (5): 1548–1555. https://doi.org/10.1021/acs.jchemed.0c01482.

Fitzgerald, F. Scott.1986. *The Great Gatsby*. First Scribner Classic/Collier Edition.

Frost, Robert. 1917. "A Servant of Servants." In North of Boston. Henry Holt and Company.

GNM Press Office. (2025, February 14). Guardian Media Group announces strategic partnership with OpenAI. *The Guardian*. https://www.theguardian.com/gnm-press-office/2025/feb/14/guardian-media-group-announces-strategic-partnership-with-openai.

Mateyka, Peter J., and Christopher R. Mazur. 2021. *Homeownership in the United States: 2005 to 2019*. American Community Survey Briefs. United States Census Bureau.

Mulach, Jordan. 2024. "Safety Authority Will Punish Carmakers for Relying on Touchscreens." *CarExpert*. March 5. https://www.carexpert.com.au/car-news/safety-authority-will-punish-carmakers-for-relying-on-touchscreens.

Naiditch, Fernando. 2010. "Critical Pedagogy and the Teaching of Reading for Social Action." *Critical Questions in Education* 1:94–107.

Reich, James. 2022. "Introducing the Ecological Uncanny." Substack newsletter. *The Ecological Uncanny*, March 15. https://jamesreich.substack.com/p/introducing-the-ecological-uncanny.

Semler, Toby, and Alex Affat. 2024. "Study Finds Physical Buttons in Cars Are Safer than Touch Screens, and Buyers Agree." *WhichCar*, March 3. https://www.whichcar.com.au/news/swedish-study-finds-physical-buttons-are-safer-than-touchscreens.

Zitron, Ed. 2023. "The Rot Economy." Ed Zitron's Where's Your Ed At, February 9. https://www.wheresyoured.at/the-rot-economy/.

Index

D. J. Gavin, *Generative AI and the Future of the Humanities*,
https://doi.org/10.1007/978-3-032-06534-6

FSC
www.fsc.org
MIX
Papier | Fördert
gute Waldnutzung
FSC® C083411

Kolibri 360 GmbH
Ferdinand-Jühlke-Straße 7
99095 Erfurt, Deutschland
produktsicherheit@kolibri360.de